MODERN BRAZIL

A Volume in the Comparative
Societies Series

MODERN BRAZIL
A Volume in the Comparative Societies Series

KEVIN NEUHOUSER
Seattle Pacific University

HAROLD R. KERBO, SERIES EDITOR
California Polytechnic State University

McGraw-Hill
College

Boston, Burr Ridge, IL Dubuque, IA Madison,WI
New York San Francisco, St. Louis
Bangkok Bogotá Caracas Lisbon London Madrid Mexico City
Milan New Delhi Seoul Singapore Sydney Taipei Toronto

McGraw-Hill College

A Division of The **McGraw·Hill** Companies

MODERN BRAZIL

This book is printed on acid-free paper.

1 2 3 4 5 6 7 8 9 0 DOC/DOC 9 3 2 1 0 9 8

ISBN 0-07-289122-X

Editorial director: *Phillip A. Butcher*
Senior sponsoring editor: *Sally Constable*
Editorial coordinator: *Amy Smeltzley*
Marketing manager: *Leslie Kraham*
Project manager: *Kimberly D. Hooker*
Production supervisor: *Scott Hamilton*
Freelance design coordinator: *Laurie J. Entringer*
Cover image: © *Stephen Simpson/FPG International LLC*
Compositor: *Shepherd, Inc.*
Typeface: *10/12 Palatino*
Printer: *R. R. Donnelley & Sons Company*

Library of Congress Cataloging-in Publication Data
Neuhouser, Kevin Leon
    Modern Brazil / Kevin Neuhouser.
       p.   cm. — (Comparative societies series)
    Includes bibliographical references and index.
    ISBN 0-07-289122-X
    1. Brazil—Social conditions.   2. Brazil—Economic
conditions—1945-   3. Brazil—Politics and government—20th century.
    I. Title.   II. Series.
HN283.5.N48   1999
306'.0981—dc21   98-12374

http://www.mhhe.com

EDITOR'S PREFACE

In one of the early scenes of the movie *Reds*, The U.S. revolutionary journalist John Reed, just back from covering the beginning of World War I, is asked by a roomful of business leaders, "What is this War really about?" John Reed stands, and stops all conversation with a one-word reply—"profits." Today, war between major industrial nations would disrupt profits much more than create money for a military industrial complex. Highly integrated global markets and infrastructures support the daily life of suburban families in Chicago and urban squatter settlements in Bombay. These ties produce a social and economic ecology that transcends political and cultural boundaries.

The world is a very different place than it was for our parents and grandparents. Those rare epic events of world war certainly invaded their everyday lives and futures, but we now find that daily events thousands of miles away, in countries large and small, have a greater impact on North Americans than ever before, with the speed of this impact multiplied many times in recent decades. Our standard of living, jobs, and even prospects of living in a healthy environment have never before been so dependent on outside forces.

Yet, there is much evidence that North Americans have less easy access to good information about the outside world than even a few years ago. Since the end of the Cold War, newspaper and television coverage of events in other countries has dropped dramatically. It is difficult to put much blame on the mass media, however: international news seldom sells any more. There is simply less interest.

It is not surprising, then, that Americans know comparatively little about the outside world. A recent *Los Angeles Times* survey provides a good example: People in eight countries were asked five basic questions about current events of the day. Americans were dead last in their knowledge, trailing people from Canada, Mexico, England, France, Spain, Germany, and Italy.* It is also not surprising that the annual report published by the Swiss World Economic Forum always ranks American executives quite low in their international experience and understanding.

Such ignorance harms American competitiveness in the world economy in many ways. But there is much more. Seymour Martin Lipset put it nicely in one of his recent books: "Those who know only one country know no country" (Lipset 1996: 17). Considerable time spent in a foreign

---

*For example, while only 3 percent of Germans missed all five questions, 37 percent of the Americans did (*Los Angeles Times*, March 16, 1994).

country is one of the best stimulants for a sociological imagination: Studying or doing research in other countries makes us realize how much we really, in fact, have learned about our own society in the process. Seeing other social arrangements, ways of doing things, and foreign perspectives allows for far greater insight to the familiar, our own society. This is also to say that ignorance limits solutions to many of our own serious social problems. How any Americans, for example, are aware that levels of poverty are much lower in all other advanced nations and that the workable government services in those countries keep poverty low? Likewise, how many Americans are aware of alternative means of providing health care and quality education or reducing crime?

We can take heart in the fact that sociology in the United States has become more comparative in recent decades. A comparative approach, of course, was at the heart of classical European sociology during the 1800s. But as sociology was transported from Europe to the United States early in the 20th century, it lost much of this comparative focus. In recent years, sociology journals have published more comparative research. There are large data sets with samples from many countries around the world in research seeking general laws on issues such as the causes of social mobility or political violence, all very much in the tradition of Durkheim. But we also need much more of the old Max Weber. His was a qualitative historical and comparative perspective (Smelser 1976; Ragin and Zaret 1983). Weber's methodology provides a richer understanding of other societies, a greater recognition of the complexity of social, cultural, and historical forces shaping each society. Ahead of his time in many ways, C. Wright Mills was planning a qualitative comparative sociology of world regions just before his death in 1961 (Horowitz 1983: 324). [Too few American sociologists have yet to follow in his footsteps.]

Following these trends, sociology textbooks in the United States have also become more comparative in content in recent years. And while this tendency must be applauded, it is not enough. Typically there is an example from Japan here, another from Germany there, and so on haphazardly for a few countries in different subject areas as the writer's knowledge of these bits and pieces allows. What we need are the textbook equivalents of a richer Weberian comparative analysis, a qualitative comparative analysis of the social, cultural, and historical forces that have combined to make relatively unique societies around the world. It is this type of comparative material that can best help people in the United States overcome their lack of understanding about other countries and allow them to see their own society with much greater insight.

The Comparative Societies Series, of which this book is a part, has been designed as a small step in filling this need. We have currently selected 12 countries on which to focus: Japan, Thailand, Switzerland, Mexico, Eritria, Hungary, Germany, China, India, Iran, Brazil, and Russia. We selected these countries as representatives of major world regions and cultures, and each will be examined in separate books written by talented sociologists. All of the basic sociological issues and topics will be covered: Each book will begin with a look at the important historical and geographical forces shaping the society, then turn to basic aspects of social organization and culture. From there each book will proceed to examine the political and economic institutions of the specific country, along with the social stratification, the family, religion, education, and finally urbanization, demography, social problems, and social change.

Although each volume in the Comparative Societies Series is of necessity brief to allow for use as supplementary readings in standard sociology courses, we have tried to assure that this brief coverage provides students with sufficient information to better understand each society, as well as their own. The ideal would be to transport every student to another country for a period of observation and learning. Realizing the unfortunate impracticality of this ideal, we hope to do the next best thing— to at least mentally move these students to a country very different from their own, provide something of the everyday reality of the people in these other countries, and demonstrate how the tools of sociological analysis can help them see these societies as well as their own with much greater understanding.

Harold R. Kerbo
San Luis Obispo, CA
June 1997

AUTHOR'S PREFACE

Despite its nearness and importance, Brazil is relatively unfamiliar to Americans. Images of Amazonian rain forests, Carnival in Rio, or World Cup soccer may flash through our minds, but perhaps little else. This is unfortunate; there is much to learn from Brazil because it is similar to the United States, yet it is fascinatingly unique. A vast country with enormous natural resources, Brazil retains the spirit of the frontier, discovery, and progress, as well as a drive to dominate nature and indigenous peoples. It was a slave society, yet it created a new culture out of the contributions of many different ethnic groups. Brazilian society is highly unequal but rapidly industrializing; it is historically Catholic but increasingly Protestant. Examining these similarities and differences not only helps us understand Brazil but also helps us understand ourselves.

Writing a book is a collective task, and I am indebted to many people for making it possible. Among those who most deserve thanks: my parents, who taught me that understanding requires curiosity and compassion; Rodolfo and Elza, who introduced me to Brazil and made me feel at home; the residents of Caranguejo, who welcomed me and taught me to see Brazil from below; Ricardo and Dona da Paz, who adopted me into their family; my Brazilian sister Wilma, who patiently answers every silly sociological question; Rebecca and Joshua, my children, who endured my constant trips to Brazil without complaint and renew my hope for the future; and Marian, my life companion since we fell in love on a Brazilian beach, who shares my passion for Brazil and its wonderful people. I also would like to thank Barbara M. Hall, who patiently worked with me to create the map of Brazil that I carry in my head.

Kevin Neuhouser

CONTENTS

MODERN BRAZIL

A Volume in the Comparative
Societies Series

MODERN BRAZIL

A Volume in the Comparative Societies Series

Brazil:
Regional Diversity

Legend:
- State capitals
- State boundaries
- Cultural Regions
  - Northeastern coast
  - Southern coast
  - Sertão
  - Agricultural heartland
  - Amazon

Source: Neuhouser (1997).

© Barbara M. Hall and W. Scott Moore 1998

Source: Neuhouser (1997).

CHAPTER 1

Sociology and Brazil

Brazil turned me into a sociologist. It didn't happen all at once, but it did begin right away. I was 16 when I first went to Brazil. Stepping off the plane, I encountered a world where much of what I had learned growing up didn't seem to apply. Eating everything on my plate meant that I was still hungry. Walking down the street with a male friend's arm around my shoulder didn't mean either of us was gay. Knowing I have light skin wasn't enough to know my race, because facial appearance, economic status, and even social relationships were as significant as skin color.

CHAMPAGNE, CUTOFFS, AND *FAVELAS*

My crash course in Brazil began when I was taken from the airport to a restaurant where my host family ordered drinks. The waiter placed a bottle in front of me, but the only word on the label that I recognized was *champagne.* You can imagine my surprise, then, to see even small children chugging straight from the bottle. It turned out that the amber liquid wasn't champagne; it wasn't even alcoholic. It was a soft drink made from *guarana,* an Amazonian berry. The label for this particular brand boasted that theirs was "the champagne of *guaranas!*"

Not all confusions were so easily cleared up. One day as I was leaving the house, my host mother began crying. After calming down, she told me that she was upset because of my clothes. I was wearing cutoff jeans—nothing unusual for an American teenager in hot weather; but she was worried that people in the community would think that she wasn't taking proper care of me. After all, my cutoffs were unraveling; they weren't even hemmed. At the time, I thought that she was overreacting, but later I learned that her response was reasonable given that in Brazilian society clothes are a critical marker of **class** status, signaling others how to treat you. Having grown up in small midwestern towns with minimal economic **stratification,** I had been blissfully ignorant of what my clothes communicated.

The most profound experience of that year in Brazil occurred near the end. Before I could return to the United States, I had to drop off my passport in São Paulo to get an exit visa. The bus left my interior town late in the evening. Early the next morning as the bus entered the city, I woke and looked out the window. I thought that I was still dreaming. Off on the horizon was a huge concentration of high-rise apartment and office buildings, but between the bus and the skyscrapers were thousands of shacks jammed together and made of odds and ends of wood, plastic, and tile. Faces flashed by—a child brushing her teeth, a woman carrying water on her head, a man loading a cart. I watched mesmerized, but I barely had time to wonder who these people were and why they were living there before the bus left them behind.

The following week, I returned to São Paulo to pick up my passport. I made sure to be wide awake as the bus approached the city, but this time there were no shacks. The field had been bulldozed clear. All that remained of those thousands of homes were mounds of smoldering rubbish. What had happened? Where were all the people, and why had their homes been demolished?

SOCIOLOGY AND BRAZIL

I couldn't get these questions, and others like them, out of my head. Brazil had opened my eyes to the amazing diversity of human behavior, but it was a diversity I didn't really understand. In college, however, I found in sociology the tools to begin answering my questions. I discovered that throughout the cities of the Third World, poor people, unable to purchase adequate housing, invade unused land and establish squatter settlements (in Brazil called *favelas*). I also learned that many governments view these poor communities as obstacles to **development,** so they frequently are removed to make room for apartment buildings, factories, and shopping centers.

So my fascinations with sociology and Brazil have grown up together. After graduating from college with a degree in sociology, I returned to Brazil to do **applied sociology** with a development **nongovernmental organization (NGO).** For three years I lived and worked in Caranguejo, a *favela* in Recife, Brazil, doing community organizing through a housing reconstruction project. After that experience, I earned a Ph.D. in sociology, writing a dissertation on the patterns of transitions between democratic and authoritarian regimes in Brazil and other South American countries. Since then, I have returned to Recife to study grassroots community mobilization. Unexpectedly, this study led me to focus on **gender** when it became clear that women rather than men were the primary activists. Thus, sociology has expanded my understanding and appreciation for Brazil, while Brazil has given me a reason to be a sociologist.

TO KNOW

In Portuguese there are two words that are translated in English as "to know." *Saber* means to know a fact objectively; *conhecer* means to know something experientially, subjectively. Thus, I can know facts about Brazil (*saber*) and I can know Brazil through personal experience (*conhecer*). This book is written to promote both types of knowing. The reader will learn specific information about Brazil and sociology, but I also hope to convey some sense of the experience of Brazil and of doing sociology because both experiences have enriched my life.

Sociology strives for objective knowledge—knowledge that is unbiased and confirmed by testing—but it also recognizes that complete objectivity is unattainable. Inevitably, we see the world from a particular point of view. To minimize the distortion that comes with every viewpoint, we must examine our perspective, to understand how it shapes what we see as well as what we can't see. To be honest, then, sociologists must be clear about the viewing point from which they observe the world.

My viewing point for Brazil is fundamentally shaped by the three years that I lived in the *favela* in Recife and the research that I've conducted there in the years since. Thus, my perception of Brazil comes from viewing it from the bottom up. Because this book is grounded in my research and experience with the urban poor, aspects of Brazil that I know less directly, such as rural Brazil or upper-class Brazilian society, inevitably receive less attention and will be relatively hidden from view. Although there are many other ways to view Brazil, the country certainly cannot be understood without this perspective because most Brazilians are urban and unfortunately most of them are poor. And while those at the top of society find it relatively easy to communicate their points of view, my friends and neighbors in the *favela* are rarely heard.

TWO INTERPRETATIONS OF BRAZIL

To understand a social reality as complex as Brazil, sociologists want as much information from as many different perspectives as possible. Large masses of unorganized information, however, can confuse more than enlighten, so sociologists develop concepts and theories that help them recognize and explain general patterns. Throughout the book, readers will be introduced to these sociological concepts and theories to help make sense of the information. Not all sociologists agree, though, on which theories are most appropriate for understanding Brazil. The most basic debate has been over the interpretation of the macro changes Brazil has undergone in the five centuries since the Portuguese conquest.

One theoretical perspective, **modernization theory,** interprets Brazilian history as the long, difficult struggle to become a modern society in the image of the United States or Japan. There may be social costs, such as the displacement of human workers by machines, but the long-term outcome will be a more prosperous and democratic Brazil. Processes like **urbanization** and industrialization are interpreted positively as evidence that Brazil is becoming modern. Negative things like democratic instability or environmental degradation are viewed as temporary. Modernization, it is believed, may create problems, but it also will create the solutions. Nations further along in the process can help with technology and investment capital, but how quickly Brazil becomes modern ultimately is determined by its own commitment to progress (Harrison 1985; Rostow 1990). This belief in modernization is officially emblazoned on the Brazilian flag—"Order and Progress."

A second major theoretical perspective, **dependency theory,** interprets the Brazilian experience very differently. Historically, colonial economic and political **structures** were established not to benefit or develop Brazil, but to enrich Portugal. As a result, Brazilian development was distorted in ways that have been extremely difficult to overcome. The export economy created incredible wealth for a very small **elite,** but it also created tremendous poverty. To stabilize this exploitative system, which required the coercion of vast numbers of workers, political power also was concentrated in the hands of the elite. These economic and political structures of domination and exploitation have persisted despite significant changes. Thus, even though Brazil has industrialized and urbanized, it has not done so in the same way that early industrializing countries like England and the United States did. Widespread poverty and vulnerability to fluctuations in the international economy continue to plague Brazil (Cardoso and Faletto 1979; Kay 1989).

Which perspective is right? Sociologists disagree, as do Brazilians. It's interesting that modernization theory was developed by European and North American theorists looking at the data from the outside, whereas the dependency perspective was developed by Latin American insiders, including the current president of Brazil, sociologist Fernando Henrique Cardoso. From the perspective of the *favela,* the dependency perspective seems to explain best the persistence of urban poverty despite rapid economic growth. Although I have my own point of view, I will present, as objectively as possible, a wide variety of findings by both Brazilian and American sociologists on the fundamental processes and institutions of Brazilian society so that readers have enough information to begin to form their own opinions. In the final chapter, I will return to this big question about how to understand Brazilian society.

MAKING THEORY REAL

To ensure that Brazil doesn't become obscured by a focus on the theories and concepts through which it is viewed, in the chapters that follow I will introduce my *favela* community and the people who live there to see what they can teach. You will meet people like Dona Nenê, who police described as "worse than a man" because of the tenacity with which she fought for housing for her family; Gilson, who was so desperate for employment that he worked for free; and Luis the thief, who lived quietly in the community until the police shot him and his body ended up behind my house. You also will be introduced to famous Brazilians like Chico Mendes, the martyred leader of the Amazon rubber tappers; Lula, the metalworker who on two occasions was nearly elected president (in informal Brazil even presidential candidates are known by their first names); and Leonardo Boff, a Franciscan priest who was silenced by the Vatican.

Getting to know individual Brazilians—some famous, some not—is essential because in them we can begin to see how geography, culture, economics, and politics come together to shape the lives of real people. These individuals are more than numbers in a census table, more than data to be explained by theory. They are people who struggle to create meaningful and joyous lives with the cultural and material resources they find around them. Sociology can help us understand this struggle, identifying the constraints and possibilities Brazilians face. In understanding Brazilians better, we begin to understand ourselves better too, seeing ourselves from a new (Brazilian) angle. After all, the struggle for meaning and joy is both the common and the infinitely varied struggle of all people in all cultures. Thus, in learning *about* Brazilians, we can learn *from* them and perhaps learn *how* to cooperate in our common struggle to be human.

CHAPTER 2

Brazil in Place and Time

Is God Brazilian? I was enjoying a day at the beach when a Brazilian friend turned to me with an expression of utter contentment and said, *"Deus é Brasileiro,"* God is Brazilian. I looked around at the blue sky, the shimmering white sand, the graceful coconut palms, the warm green waves crashing over coral reefs . . . paradise.

If God is Brazilian, then God must love tropical beaches as much as Brazilians do. The beach I was lying on stretches for more than 3,000 miles—from French Guiana in the north to Uruguay in the south—and approximately 80 percent of all Brazilians live within about 200 miles of the coast (Burns 1993: 476). On sunny weekends the beaches are packed with Brazilians swimming, playing soccer, eating, drinking, and soaking up the sun.

Why begin a sociological analysis of Brazil by discussing geography? Sociologists frequently ignore the impact of the physical environment on social behavior, but culture, economy, and politics are all shaped by the resources and constraints of the physical environment. Three thousand miles of tropical beaches impact Brazil—from how Brazilians spend their leisure time to how they earn their living. Less obvious is that culture, economy, and politics also impact the physical environment. Brazilians' passion for a lifestyle of sun and sand has transformed the coastline; isolated fishing villages have been replaced by crowded hotels and restaurant-lined promenades. To begin to understand Brazil sociologically, we need to understand how Brazil has been created through the interaction of humans with their physical environment.

Brazil, however, did not emerge out of this interaction all at once; it is the product of a historical process, as Brazilians adapted and readapted to an environment that they continually transformed. The patterns of land and resource exploitation initiated 500 years ago by the early Portuguese colonizers established amazingly durable political and economic **structures.** These colonial legacies must be analyzed, then, in order to develop a sociological understanding of modern Brazil.

BRAZIL AS HISTORICAL PLACE

Brazil is huge—the fifth largest country in the world, larger than the continental United States and covering half of South America. (Table 2–1 shows various world rankings of Brazil.) Roughly diamond-shaped, it stretches about 2,700 miles north to south and east to west. The country straddles the equator; all of Brazil lies within the tropics except for a few states in the far south. Only in the far south does it get cold enough for an occasional snowfall.

When Americans think of Brazil, the first thing that comes to mind is Amazonia; at least this is the **stereotype** Brazilians have of Americans. Most Brazilians, though, view the Amazon as peripheral to the rest of the country, much like many Americans think of Alaska—distant, inhospitable, and significant only for its natural beauty and mineral resources.

Brazilians divide their country into two culturally distinct regions: the *litoral* (coast) and the interior. Coastal residents generally think of the interior as backward, rural, and poor and the coast as modern, urban, and culturally sophisticated. Predictably, residents of the interior see things differently; they view the coast as crowded, chaotic, and polluted and characterize the interior as having open spaces, where people live secure in the familiarity of traditional communities.

A major factor in the emergence of these two cultural regions is the low coastal mountain range that separates them. In Rio de Janeiro, the mountains come down right to the beaches, providing one of the most spectacular urban settings in the world. Although beautiful, these mountains presented a communication and transportation barrier between the coast and the interior. Only two rivers—the Amazon in the far north and the São Francisco in the northeast—link the interior to the coast, but neither serves major industrial or population centers. For much of Brazil's

TABLE 2–1

Brazil: World Rankings

	Number	World Rank	Year
Population	147 million	6th	1991
Territory	8.6 million km²	5th	1995
GDP (gross domestic product)	$US 414 billion	10th	1991
Vehicles reduction	1.6 million	9th	1994
Steel production	28 million tons	7th	1991
World Cup soccer titles	4	1st	1997
Infant mortality	5.7% live births	137th	1990–95
Population growth	1.6% annually	74th	1990–95
University faculty	41% female	10th	1990

Source: UN (1995); Schneider (1996); Shapiro (1996); Coelho (1997).

White sand and coconut palm trees make Brazil's beaches some of the most beautiful in the world. In urban areas, the beaches are lined with high-rise apartment buildings, which are home to the Brazilian elite.

history, then, the interior has been relatively remote and isolated from the major coastal cities.

Neither the coast nor the interior is homogeneous; each contains diverse natural and social environments. The interior has three major subregions: the Amazon rain forest, the dry northeastern *sertão*, and the agricultural heartland of the center and south. The coast has two major subregions: the sugar-growing northeast and the industrial south.

THE NORTHEAST COAST

On March 8, 1500, Pedro Cabral set out for India with 1,200 men on 13 ships. Sailing south along the coast of Africa, the ships were pushed off course by adverse winds and currents until on April 22, land was unexpectedly sighted to the west. Unaware that he had landed on the continent of South America (present-day southern Bahia), Cabral claimed the "island" of Vera Cruz for the Portuguese crown. The fleet quickly departed for the profits of India when no evidence of gold or valuable spices was detected.

The Portuguese, however, soon discovered a lucrative resource, which was also the origin of the name of their territory: brazilwood, a tree containing a valuable red dye. To fend off foreign competitors, Portugal encouraged **colonization.** Brazil was divided into 15 "captaincies," averaging 150 miles of coastline and extending westward as far as the ill-defined line of Tordesillas separating Spanish and Portuguese territorial claims. The crown donated the captaincies to individuals who were responsible for their colonization and development. The outlines of some captaincies still can be discerned in the boundaries of northeastern states.

The captaincy system had two critical long-term consequences. First, the captaincies initiated a pattern of land concentration, in which a few families controlled the principle source of wealth. As a result, Brazil has been plagued by huge economic inequalities. According to the World Bank, Brazil has the worst income inequality in the world (Hoffman 1989). Land concentration also led to the widespread use of **coerced labor**—primarily slavery—to work the large plantations.

Second, the captaincies created a political system in which the large landowners assumed governmental responsibilities such as the maintenance of public order, definition of laws and their applicability, and the appointment of government officials. Because of the power of the large landowners, government in Brazil has been relatively weak, unable to address the social problems arising from land concentration. Powerful landowners have successfully blocked every attempt at meaningful **land reform** even though land redistribution would reduce rural poverty and stem the overwhelming flow of peasants into the Amazon and the coastal cities.

These two problems are most pronounced along the northeast coast where the captaincy system was implemented. The coastal *fazendeiros* (large landowners) quickly discovered that the region's rich soils were perfect for producing something Europeans craved: sugar (Mintz 1985). The Portuguese initially used Indian workers to grow and process the sugarcane, but those that did not succumb to European illnesses like measles and smallpox frequently escaped into the vast interior of the continent.

To satisfy the demand for workers, the Portuguese imported slaves. Over the next three centuries, an estimated 3.5 million Africans were violently transported to Brazil, six times the number entering the United States. Throughout the northeast, but especially in the port cities of Recife, Pernambuco, and Salvador, Bahia (the colonial capital), slaves imparted a strong African flavor to the **culture.** Much of what makes Brazilian culture distinct comes from Africa, from the way Portuguese is spoken to the practice of a unique form of Catholicism.

The northeast coastal cities were administrative centers for the captaincies and centers of trade with Portugal. Political and economic power, however, resided elsewhere. Trade was controlled by the Portuguese crown, and *fazendeiros* held political control of the countryside. Thus, the cities presented a rich facade as they captured some of the sugar profits that flowed through them, but no real economic development took place because neither the crown nor the landowners would have benefited from agricultural diversification or the creation of local industry.

Portugal monopolized trade with Brazil in order to extract as much profit as possible. To prevent Brazil from becoming self-sufficient (no longer needing to import goods from Portugal), Portugal prohibited industrialization in the colony. Unable to invest in industry and not needing to invest in more efficient agricultural technology because of the protected Portuguese market, sugar growers wasted their profits on conspicuous consumption of imported luxury goods. In 1639, for example, an estimated 25 percent of all the profits from the sugar crop were spent on imported French wine (Hewlett 1980).

For 450 years, the rich soils of the northeast coast have produced great quantities of sugar, yet the economy has remained largely stagnant. Even after Brazil gained independence from Portugal, little changed as the sugar growers retained their power and found it cheaper to import manufactured goods from England than to invest in local industry. The region produced enormous profits for others but never developed economically. Thus, northeastern cities remain the poorest in all Brazil, with average poverty rates at about 40 percent, twice the level of cities in southern Brazil (ETAPAS 1991).

If anything, the poverty in the rural sugarcane zone is worse, with lower wages and less access to education and health care. Despite rich soils, the rural population suffers from chronic malnutrition and hunger. Unable to grow food because the land is planted in sugarcane and unable to buy adequate food because of appallingly low wages (the average northeastern rural worker earns less than 30 percent of the national average), sugarcane workers have an average daily intake of only 1,500 to 1,700 calories, slightly lower than the average intake of prisoners at Buchenwald concentration camp (Scheper-Hughes 1992). The most obvious consequence is stunted growth; less obvious is the lack of energy and resistance to disease (Castro 1992).

The Brazilian government recognized the economic and social problems of the region and created a federal agency in 1959—SUDENE—to promote economic development. SUDENE has stimulated industrialization and increased mechanization of agriculture, but overall it has had little impact on the region's poverty. Thus, despite its importance during the colonial period, the northeast coast lags far behind the rapidly expanding economies of Brazil's other regions—all other regions, that is, except the *sertão*.

THE *SERTÃO*

Inland from the northeast coast is the dry and desolate *sertão*. Indians called the thorn-infested scrub forest *caatinga*, or "white forest," because of the lack of any green during much of the year. This inhospitable region, about 10 percent of the country, is surprisingly densely populated. During the colonial period, the *sertão* provided cattle and leather goods for the coast as well as sanctuary for escaped slaves and anyone else seeking to avoid the social controls of the more-settled coast.

The geographic and social isolation of the *sertão* hides its poverty. Endemic malnutrition stunts the physical development of the children who don't contribute to the appallingly high infant **mortality rate.** The United Nations has estimated that daily caloric intake is less than 80 percent of the recommended level; another study found that *sertanejos* receive only half the required amount of vitamin A (Page 1995). As a result, the average **life expectancy** was reported to have been as low as 30 years in some areas as recently as the early 1960s (Castro 1992), though life expectancy has slowly risen since then.

Enough rain falls in good years to allow inhabitants to eke out a livelihood, but drought periodically devastates the *sertão*. In the drought of 1790–93, one-third of the inhabitants of Pernambuco state died; the great drought of 1877–79 cut the population of Ceará in half. While I was living in Recife, the *sertão* experienced perhaps the worst drought of the 20th century (1979–83), affecting up to 10 million people and causing the deaths of between 250,000 and one million people (Page 1995).

Outsiders have difficulty comprehending the intense love that *sertanejos* have for their harsh homeland. When drought hits, most inhabitants stay, reciting prayer upon prayer, hoping against hope that rain will come in time to save their livestock and to allow them to plant fields. When the rain fails to appear, they are weak and malnourished, making exodus to the coast a deadly imperative. The arrival in the coastal cities of the emaciated survivors of the death march—"with blackened skin glued to their bones"(Scheper-Hughes 1992)—has seared the memories and imaginations of Brazilians and inspired some of Brazil's greatest literary work. *Rebellion in the Backlands* by Euclides da Cunha (1957) and *Barren Lives* by Graciliano Ramos (1969), for example, have won international acclaim.

The arrival of *sertanejos* inflated the urban populations of the northeast coast, but millions also migrated far to the south, primarily to São Paulo. The cities were ill-prepared to receive them; so many are **underemployed,** forced to live in the ever-growing urban *favelas*. Imagine the culture shock of people who see the ocean for the very first time after fleeing a drought, who move into densely populated *favelas* after life in the isolation of the *sertão*. It's not surprising that many migrants stay only until they hear news of rain, upon which they abandon the city's "advantages" for the *sertão*'s hardships.

Nature is not the *sertanejos*' only adversary. The *sertão* is dominated by the "colonels," *fazendeiros* whose military titles come from control of private armies. Colonels control the *sertão*'s two critical resources (water and land), which gives them political control. To access these resources, peasants enter into **patron–client relations** with the colonels. Ideally, the **client** gives labor and loyalty to the **patron** in exchange for protection, land, and water. In practice, the colonels often take advantage of the dependent peasants.

Antagonism to the colonels runs deep, sometimes erupting in dramatic opposition. The *sertão* is famous for its bandits (Pang 1989), like

Lampião (1898–1938), who reacted to personal injustices by entering into lives of crime, stealing from the rich who had oppressed them. Admired by the poor who received gifts of stolen goods, they were recognized by those in power as much more threatening than ordinary criminals. As one newspaper proclaimed in 1878, "These bandits loot properties in the most unrestricted fashion as if communism had already been proclaimed among us" (Burns 1993: 301).

The *sertão*'s harsh social and physical environment also generated **messianic movements,** groups of people looking for a savior to initiate an era of justice and righteousness. Portuguese settlers told the story of King Sebastian who disappeared in 1578 while fighting the infidel Moors in north Africa. According to legend, he didn't die but awaits the right time to return and rescue his people (Vita 1991). Many *sertanejos* believed that the end times had begun when the Brazilian monarchy was overthrown in 1889, followed by the separation of church and state (1891) and the imposition of new taxes by the secular government.

In 1893, under the leadership of Antônio Conselheiro, *sertanejos* flocked to Canudos, a very remote area in the state of Bahia, to build a "new Jerusalem." At its peak, Canudos may have been home to as many as 30,000 people. The motivation was overtly religious (so they were labeled "fanatics"), but Canudos was also a social experiment in which Conselheiro's **charismatic authority** replaced the political and economic control of the colonels and the religious authority of the Catholic Church. Thus, it wasn't long before the community came under attack.

In 1896, three army expeditions were defeated by Conselheiro's followers, who compensated for the lack of modern weapons with guerrilla tactics and superior knowledge of harsh local conditions. Humiliated, the government dispatched 8,000 soldiers, three generals, and the minister of war to lay siege to Canudos. Vicious fighting ended with house-to-house combat as the *sertanejos* refused to surrender. The government's victory was costly—5,000 soldiers and 15,000 civilians were killed (Burns 1993; Schneider 1996). Sadly, the attack on Canudos is eerily similar to the U.S. government's response to David Koresh and his followers in Waco, Texas.

Messianic movements did not end with Canudos. At about the same time, Padre Cicero was drawing followers to Juazeiro in the *sertão* of Paraiba. More pragmatic than Counselheiro, Padre Cicero negotiated an uneasy accommodation with the political authorities, though he was suspended from the priesthood. Since Cicero's death, Juazeiro has become the most important center of religious pilgrimage in the region. Packed into the backs of trucks, tens of thousands of devotees of Padre Cicero go every year to seek help and to keep promises for past favors.

It is not surprising that, helpless in the face of a harsh climate and powerless in the hands of the colonels, *sertanejos* seek help in the supernatural. Even the government's efforts to solve regional problems often reinforced existing inequities. So much government money has been spent to increase the water supply (wells, reservoirs, water trucks) and so many of those efforts have benefited the colonels that it is known in Brazil as the *industria da seca* (the drought industry). Typically, the reservoirs and wells are built on the colonels' property to water their livestock and irrigate their crops, while poor *sertanejos* still lack secure sources of water for themselves and their subsistence farms. Thus, despite the introduction of modern infrastructure like paved roads and electricity, the *sertão* remains much the same as it was in colonial times.

THE AMAZON

Northwest of the arid *sertão*, the rain-forested Amazon covers two million square miles and over 40 percent of the national territory. The region is named for the Amazon River, which originates only a hundred miles from the Pacific Ocean (18,000 feet up in the Peruvian Andes) but flows to the Atlantic 4,000 miles away. Unbelievably immense, the Amazon carries 20 percent of all the fresh water flowing into all the oceans of the world (170 billion gallons per hour), 14 times more water than the Mississippi. The Amazon is so massive that at its mouth it contains an island—Marajó—larger than Switzerland (Revkin 1990; Schneider 1996).

The biological diversity of the Amazon is no less astounding than its size. In 1983, it was estimated that the region contained one million species of plants and animals; more recent estimates top 10 to 15 million. Diverse temperate forests have fewer than 25 species of trees; but in just one 2.5-acre site outside Manaus, 414 tree species have been identified. A single tree yielded 1,500 insect species (Revkin 1990).

Despite stunning natural abundance, the Amazon always has been sparsely populated. Today, 17 million people live in the region, but 10 million are urban. "There are probably no more people living in the forest today than there were at the time of the European invasion in the 16th century" (*New Internationalist* 1995: 102). The fertility of the Amazon actually is a mirage. The soils are ancient and nutrient poor; agronomists only classify 4 percent as fertile. **Indigenous populations** successfully farmed the Amazon for thousands of years with slash-and-burn techniques—shifting to new plots every few years, allowing the rain forest to reclaim old plots. Modern, large-scale attempts at permanent farming in the Amazon, however, generally have produced disastrous results. Production is low and risks desertification as clear-cutting, burning, and erosion overwhelm the fragile ecosystem (Revkin 1990). Figure 2–1 charts Amazonian deforestation since 1500.

The stress on the Amazon likely will continue for two reasons. First, the region contains an abundance of valuable mineral resources. More gold is being extracted from the Amazon than was produced during the California gold rush. At one site—Serra Pelada—14 tons of gold were extracted in a single year (1983). Hunting these riches are an estimated 300,000 gold miners. Unfortunately, to extract gold many of them use mercury; as much as 3,000 tons may have been dumped into

FIGURE 2–1

Amazonian Deforestation Since 1500

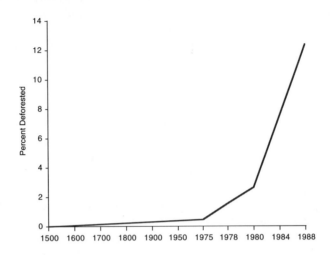

Source: Pearce & Myers (1990: 386).

Amazonian rivers since 1950 (Page 1995). The mercury is absorbed by fish, which then are eaten by the region's inhabitants, causing a potentially fatal deterioration of the nervous system.

Gold isn't the only valuable mineral resource. In 1967, the largest deposit of high-grade iron ore (18 billion tons) was discovered at Carajás; the 400,000-acre site also contains copper (1.2 billion tons), manganese (60 million tons), and bauxite ore (4.1 billion tons). In addition to this partial list of the unimaginable mineral wealth are one million tons of gold. To exploit these deposits, the Brazilian government received $4.9 billion from the World Bank; Japan and Europe invested another $1.05 billion. As a result, the nearby town of Marabá mushroomed from 10,000 residents in the 1950s to 200,000 by the late 1980s (Davis 1977; Cleary 1990; Barbosa 1993a, 1993b). As the Brazilian government promotes the exploitation of the Amazon's mineral resources to fuel economic growth, population and environmental pressures will only intensify.

The second major source of ecological pressure is the government's promotion of agriculture. Millions of landless peasants have migrated to the coastal cities, generating crowding and unemployment. The government, under the slogan "land without people for people without land," responded with colonization schemes to divert migrants to the Amazon. Although these small farmers used slash-and-burn methods, their numbers and failure to rotate garden plots threaten the fragile rain forest.

The government, however, believed that the Amazon was so immense that small farmers were insufficient to tap its agricultural potential, so it offered large tax breaks to corporations that invested in the Amazon. Response was immediate. Orlando Ometo, for example, a large sugar producer, bought 5,000 square miles of land (bigger than Connecticut) to graze cattle (Davis 1977). Although cattle ranching is a principle cause of deforestation, the Amazon remains a net importer of beef because clearing pasture is used more to claim land and tax breaks than to actually produce meat (*New Internationalist* 1995).

The best-known megalandholding was the four million acres on the Jari River purchased by American billionaire Daniel Keith Ludwig for just $3 million in 1967. Ludwig floated a Japanese wood-pulp plant across the Pacific and then up the Amazon. Disease and insects, however, kept destroying the imported trees that Ludwig planted in large fields cleared of the diverse native species. After 15 years and an investment of nearly $1 billion with little return, Ludwig sold out to a consortium of Brazilian investors at a huge loss (Barbosa 1993b; Page 1995).

In response to the destruction, indigenous groups and *seringueiros* (rubber tappers who have harvested the rain forest with sustainable methods for generations) have joined together to protect the Amazon. They invented the strategy of *empates*—standoffs in which they confront and disarm chainsaw-wielding crews sent to clear the forest.

Chico Mendes became the symbol of this struggle. A *seringueiro* from the state of Acre, Chico was instrumental in developing the concept of *extractive reserves*:

> legally protected tracts of rainforest from which sustainably harvestable non-timber forest products . . . are collected and marketed. . . While the land is owned by the Brazilian government, the products of extraction are managed by, and benefit, local communities (La Tour 1995: 123).

Despite past conflict, rubber tappers and Indians have united around a common interest in the extractive reserves and against the specter of rain forest destruction. The concept of extractive reserves also laid the basis for an international alliance with environmental organizations attracted to a strategy that could preserve the rain forest without denying the rights of local inhabitants to make a living.

As the movement grew, its impact was felt from remotest Amazonia to the national capital in Brasília and even in the halls of the World Bank. Threatened, *fazendeiros* reacted violently. Three days before Christmas 1988, Chico was murdered as he stepped out the backdoor of his house. According to the Catholic Church's Pastoral Land Commission, 1,658 people were killed in land disputes from 1968 to 1991, but only 5 people were convicted for these crimes (Perney 1995: 109). It was probably due to Chico's international reputation that a local landowner and his son were actually found guilty of the murder. They did not remain in jail for long, however, cutting through the bars of their cell window and escaping, probably into Bolivia with the collusion of local authorities (Page 1995). One of Chico's murderers was recaptured in 1996 and remains in jail.

During the 1970s, deforestation averaged about 13,600 km^2, but by the late 1980s had risen to 50–80,000 km^2 annually (Skole and Tucker 1993). The worst year may have been 1987 when "an exceptionally dry burning season, and landowners, fearing agrarian reform, wanted to secure their claim to the land" (*New Internationalist* 1995: 102). In the early 1990s, the deforestation rate appeared to fall as pressure from the Indians, rubber tappers, and environmentalists has begun to impact governmental policies and development agencies like the World Bank. Thus, some tax incentives for cattle ranching were eliminated and some environmental safeguards for mining operations were enacted. In 1995, however, deforestation rose sharply and remained at high levels in 1996–97 (Astor 1997).

Events in the Amazon have fueled debate over the idea of **sustainable development,** which the World Commission on Environment and Development defines as "development that meets the needs of the present without compromising the ability of future generations to meet their own needs" (quoted in Smith and Young 1998: 476). For example, the extractive reserves proposed by Brazilian rubber tappers potentially allow for the economic use of the Amazon without destroying it. The feasibility of the extractive reserves, however, can't be evaluated until the pressures on the Amazon generated by economic and social problems in other regions of Brazil are solved.

THE AGRICULTURAL HEARTLAND

South of the Amazon and *sertão* and inland from the coast lies Brazil's agricultural heartland. Historically, the interior of the state of São Paulo was the center of farm production, and it still accounts for over 20 percent of Brazil's agricultural output (Schneider 1996). During the 19th century, however, the agricultural frontier moved steadily south into Paraná, Santa Catarina, and Rio Grande do Sul. Together, these states now account for over half the country's farm production.

The fertile soil and the relatively cool climate of these southern states attracted more immigrants than any other interior region. After slavery was abolished in 1888, coffee growers, especially in São Paulo, contracted large numbers of Italian and Japanese workers. Following World War I, German immigrants established agricultural colonies further to the south in Paraná and Santa Catarina. The Italians assimilated most quickly into Brazilian society, while the Germans and especially the Japanese struggled to maintain their culture and language.

The southern agricultural heartland is the most prosperous area of the Brazilian interior. In combination with the many immigrant communities, this creates a more European feel. For example, Blumenau, a dynamic city of 230,000 in Santa Catarina settled by German immigrants, has a thriving textile industry, features half-timbered architecture, and hosts an annual *Oktoberfest*. In the early 1980s, I visited an elderly German couple in Santa Catarina who after 60 years in Brazil spoke only a few words of Portuguese. But then there was little reason to learn Portuguese when their neighbors and even their mayor only spoke German.

In recent years, the southern agricultural heartland has experienced rapid mechanization as the introduction of crops like soybeans opened up new export markets. Mechanization, however, threw countless rural families out of work. Many migrated to the Amazon; many more migrated to the coastal cities; but a significant number stayed to struggle for land to feed their families. With the help of the Catholic Church, they organized the Movement of Those Without Land (MST). With the support of MST, land invasions have increased and some of the most violent conflicts have occurred in Paraná.

Expansion of the agricultural frontier northwest into Mato Grosso and Goiás initially was slower than to the south. It was so slow that the Brazilian government took the initiative to draw settlers from the coast into this vast region. In three years (1957–60), a new national capital—Brasília—was built 575 miles northeast of Rio de Janeiro, the old capital. In just two generations, a cattle pasture became the ninth largest city in the country with 1.6 million inhabitants (1991).

After Brasília's construction, highways were extended north to further draw the coastal population away from the coast. The capital was connected to Belém at the mouth of the Amazon, and another road pushed west to Cuiabá before turning north to Porto Velho in Rondônia. The resulting demographic and economic growth was so rapid that the government split both the states of Mato Grosso and Goiás in two. Brazil's most rapidly growing cities are found in this region. In 1950, Goiânia, the capital of Goiás, had only 53,000 inhabitants; by 1991 the population exceeded 900,000. Porto Velho, the capital of Rondônia, was a small town of 27,000 in 1950, but is now a dynamic city of nearly 300,000.

The southern heartland may have a European flavor, but the northern heartland is more like the traditional American wild west, complete with large cattle ranches and armed cowboys. The distance from major population centers causes a chronic shortage of workers, and some ranchers employ coercive strategies to attract and maintain their labor force. In a small town in the *sertão*, José da Silva recounted how labor recruiters appeared one day promising good wages and working conditions. Several dozen men from the town accepted the offer and set out together on the back of a truck. After several days, they arrived at the ranch only to find that they had to pay for the cost of the truck that had transported them as well as for the tools they needed to work. The men were penniless, so the costs were assessed against future wages. The debt kept growing, however, as they also had to pay for room and board. Not surprisingly, the men were unable to work off the rapidly accumulating debt, so they were kept under armed guard. Those who attempted to run away were beaten and chained to their beds or sometimes killed as a warning to other workers. José had escaped by stealing food and then hiding in the forest until pursuit died down. He was the only one from his town who had ever made it back home.

THE SOUTHERN COAST

A sharp contrast emerges while traveling south along the coast of Brazil, not in the physical environment but in the social. The northeast is poor; but the southern coast is the most prosperous region in Brazil and the manufacturing center of the entire continent. Average income in the urban south is almost twice that of cities in the northeast. Brazilian industry is concentrated within a triangle defined by the first, second, and fourth largest cities: São Paulo, Rio de Janeiro, and Belo Horizonte. Metropolitan São Paulo alone produces 25 percent of the nation's gross domestic product and is home to the world's ninth largest automobile industry. Known for tourism, Rio de Janeiro also produces petrochemicals and ships, while Belo Horizonte is home to the world's seventh largest steel industry (IBGE 1995; Page 1995; Schneider 1996; Shapiro 1996).

The cities of the southern coast are strikingly modern. In northeastern cities, the prevalence of the past is clear: 16th century cathedrals and monasteries, mansions of former slave owners, the narrow cobblestone streets of Olinda and Salvador. In the south, the colonial heritage is hidden by high-rise office and apartment buildings. São Paulo seems less like a Brazilian city than a generic modern metropolis with all the contemporary urban problems of crime, traffic congestion, and smog. Except for the sound of Portuguese, you could easily imagine yourself in New York or Chicago; on the city's subway system in the suburb of Liberdade, surrounded by Japanese-Brazilians, you might think that you are in Tokyo.

Income levels are much higher in the industrialized southern coast than elsewhere in Brazil. The region also has the highest health and educational levels in the country. Regional inequality, however, fueled massive migration from poorer areas that in some cases overwhelmed the industrial cities of the south. For example, an estimated 600,000 people migrated to São Paulo *each year* during the early 1970s (Roberts 1978). One consequence of urban growth without planning is that São Paulo may have the least green space per capita of any major city in the world. Rapid industrialization also created devastating environmental problems. A 1980 government study found that factories in the industrial city of Cubatão "were discharging 10 thousand tons of toxic gases and particulate matter into the atmosphere . . . [and] were dumping 26 tons of poisonous wastes into adjacent rivers" *every day* (Page 1995: 276–77).

Industrialization caused problems, but it also created resources that could be used to solve them. For example, between 1983 and 1990 nearly 90 percent of the identified pollution sources in Cubatão were regulated, and fish have returned to the city's rivers (Page 1995). Curitiba experienced explosive growth, doubling in size from 609,000 to 1.3 million between 1970 and 1991; but with imaginative urban planning it avoided many problems. The city's internationally recognized recycling program not only protects the environment but saves money and improves the nutrition of the poor by paying for trash collection with food. In the words of Mayor Jaime Lerner, "Curitiba proves that Brazil is possible" (Page 1995: 490).

CONCLUSION

From the rain forest jungles of the Amazon to the concrete jungles of São Paulo, from the colonial frontier of the Atlantic coast to the contemporary agricultural frontier on the borders of Peru and Bolivia, Brazil displays amazingly varied social and physical environments. Given that it is a country half a continent in size, the geographic and social diversity are not surprising. What is perhaps unexpected is that this diversity is woven together into an amazingly cohesive nation. Descendants of Indians, Europeans, Africans, and Japanese live side by side and intermarry to such an extent that their children have been described as a new "tropical race" (Freyre 1963), all of whom think of themselves as Brazilians. The chapters that follow explore some of the national institutions and shared experiences that undergird this unity.

This is not to say that Brazil is free of conflict. This chapter has introduced some of the significant, even violent, struggles over resources in Brazil. Given the extraordinarily high inequality, however, one might expect such conflicts to be much worse than they are. For example, race and class are highly correlated in Brazil, yet Brazil has never had a large race-based social movement. Regional inequalities are obvious, yet Brazil didn't experience the devastating civil wars of its Spanish-speaking neighbors. The chapters that follow explore the causes and consequences of both conflict and cohesion in Brazil.

CHAPTER 3

Race in Brazil

When I went to Brazil for the first time as a 16-year-old exchange student, I was quickly adopted into my host family. My father, Rodolfo, the son of Italian immigrants, would be considered white in the United States; my mother, Elza, because of her dark skin would be considered black. In Brazil they were neither white nor black. **Race** in Brazil is a continuum not a dichotomy (black/white), and both of my Brazilian parents were somewhere in the middle.

In Brazil there are dozens of different named positions between black and white. In a national survey, respondents asked to identify their color (Brazilians prefer the term *color* to *race*) provided 136 different terms, ranging from pale white to cinnamon brown to toasted (Coelho 1996: 270–71). Brazilians recognize subtle differences in color; how many Americans could differentiate between one person who is nut brown and another who is tanned brown?

The Brazilian system is complex not only because of the number of categories but also because skin color is not the only factor. Physical characteristics like hair color and texture, shape of the nose, and color of the eye also contribute to the determination of a person's race. Thus, two people with identical skin color are categorized differently if their overall appearance is different (Kottak 1992).

Another important element of race is class. Higher economic and social status yields a lighter classification (Lovell and Wood 1998). Identical twins with different class positions aren't identical in terms of race. The higher class twin is "whiter" than the poorer twin. This might be hard for Americans to comprehend, but there is one striking similarity with the American racial system: White is higher status than black.

The final factor determining race is social distance. The more intimate and friendly the relationship, the better known a person is, the lighter the classification. Because lighter is more valued and because appearance is so complex, people give the benefit of the doubt to someone about whom they feel positively. The opposite occurs in a socially distant relationship. Because the context of particular relationships is so important, one's race varies depending on the situation.

The fundamental dimension of the American racial system—ancestry—is absent in Brazil. In the United States, race is based on **hypodescent**—assigning a child to the race of the parent with the lower racial status. Thus, children of mixed European and African ancestry are considered to be black no matter how light their skin color (Marger 1997). In Brazil, parents' race is irrelevant; children of the same parents can all be classified differently depending on appearance, class, and social distance. There may be as many racial classifications as family members.

We usually think of race as a biological concept, categorizing individuals based on some clear physical difference; but the striking contrast between the U.S. and Brazilian racial systems reveals that race is a social construction. All of us (unless we are identical twins) are genetically unique, yet we all share basic human physical attributes as well. So why do cultures draw arbitrary lines, constructing racial categories? Racial classification often is a way to control access to important resources. In Brazil, being defined as nonwhite restricts access to education, health, and work (Lovell and Wood 1998). Thus, race is not a neutral biological concept but a socially constructed weapon in the competition for scarce resources.

INTERRACIAL MARRIAGE

To Americans, perhaps the most striking thing about my Brazilian family is not the differences in skin color but the simple fact that they are a family. In the United States, interracial marriages are becoming more common but are still relatively rare; in 1992, less than 0.5 percent of married couples in the United States were black-white couples (Schwartz and Scott 1994). The 1980 census reported that 20 percent of Brazil's marriages were interracial. Although most couples were either brown-black or brown-white, nearly 1.5 percent of all couples were black-white, three times the U.S. rate (Silva 1987). In fact, the number of black-white couples in Brazil is certainly higher than reported because marriage to a lighter-skinned person "lightens" the racial category of the partner (Telles 1993).

With so many interracial marriages, it is not surprising that many Brazilians are of mixed ancestry. The census bureau reported that in 1993, 40 percent of the population was *pardo* (brown), 5 percent was black, and 54 percent was white; less than 1 percent was indigenous or Asian (IBGE 1995). The accuracy of these numbers is disputed. White is higher status, and no intermediary categories between white and *pardo* were allowed in the census. Thus, it's likely that many light-skinned individuals of mixed ancestry responded as being white (Twine 1998: 112–15). In fact, apart from recent immigrants, there probably are few Brazilians of either purely African or European descent.

A RACIAL DEMOCRACY?

Because most Brazilians are of mixed descent and because in ordinary social interaction there is less overt racial tension than in the United States, many Brazilians claim that they live in a "racial democracy" (Freyre 1946). "Three Girls from the Same Street," a famous painting by Maria Margarida, illustrates this belief; one girl is European, one African, and one Indian. Streets with such racially diverse residents are common in Brazil. The ease with which Brazilians of all colors interact with one another is truly remarkable.

Brazilians, however, now question the belief in **racial democracy.** Rapidly accumulating data document that darker-skinned Brazilians on average are poorer, less educated, and less healthy than lighter-skinned Brazilians (Lovell and Wood 1998). The reality of racial inequality, however, hasn't stimulated the rise of a national, popular movement in Brazil to address this problem. Racial **discrimination** and **prejudice** are hidden behind a discourse of equality and an ambiguous classification system, making it difficult for dark-skinned Brazilians to mobilize (Hanchard 1994; Twine 1998). To understand Brazil's unique racial system, we must ana-lyze the three major racial groups—Indians, Europeans, and Africans—as well as the origins and consequences of a racially mixed population.

THE INDIGENOUS CONTRIBUTION

Brazil's indigenous populations are descendants of Asians who migrated to the western hemisphere 20–40,000 years ago. At the time of European contact, an estimated 80 million people lived in Latin America, but only 2–5 million within the borders of contemporary Brazil (Schwerin 1991; Burns 1993; Ribeiro 1995). In the immensity of eastern South America, this indigenous population was scattered in relatively small tribes and villages.

For the sake of simplicity, these diverse groups can be classified as belonging to two kinds of cultures. The majority had developed a tropical forest culture based on slash-and-burn agriculture, supplemented by hunting/fishing and gathering. A smaller population of seminomadic for-aging groups lived in the drier and more isolated savannas of the central interior of Brazil (Burns 1993).

Tropic Forest Cultures

Tropical forest cultures predominated throughout the Amazon and along the Atlantic coast. The peoples of the tropical forests spoke a vari-ety of related languages called *Tupí-Guaraní.* Because of their location in the first areas of European contact, the Tupí-Guaraní provided the basis for the Portuguese perception of "Indians."

Living in lush, sparsely populated regions, the Tupí-Guaraní im-pressed the Portuguese by the ease with which they produced all they needed for survival. Many domesticated plants—manioc, sweet potatoes, sugarcane, tobacco—were unknown to Europeans, but they were quickly adopted (Wearne 1996). The Portuguese were amazed by the practice of sleeping "midair" in hammocks. Travelers on Amazon riverboats and in the *sertão* still carry their own hammocks because beds often are unavailable.

The Tupí-Guaraní lived in large villages (300–2,000 inhabitants) located along the many rain forest rivers. Flooding during the rainy season ensured the fertility of their garden plots. The rivers also provided fish and a convenient place to bathe. The Tupí-Guaraní practice of bathing several times a day impressed the Europeans, but probably no more than the Tupí-Guaraní were impressed that the Portuguese bathed just several times a year. Fortunately, the Portuguese adopted the Tupí-Guaraní practice.

When the Portuguese arrived on the Brazilian coast, they encountered people who without embarrassment wore minimal clothing and worked much less than Europeans because of the efficiency of their food production. To the Portuguese, the Tupí-Guaraní seemed to be innocent children living in a tropical garden of Eden. This view changed quickly, however, when the Tupí-Guaraní resisted conversion to Catholicism and refused to work for the Portuguese. They still seemed childlike, but now they were acting like disobedient and rebellious children, requiring the firm discipline of Portuguese authority.

The Tupí-Guaraní resisted European invasion in every way possible. Although individual tribes won some battles, they never consolidated their success by cooperating in multitribe alliances. Confronted by a united enemy with superior military technology, armed resistance ultimately proved futile. Those who survived fled inland to isolated regions of the Amazon basin.

Resisting enslavement and forced conversion, many died fighting the Portuguese; more died under the terrible conditions of **coerced labor.** The majority, however, died in devastating epidemics that swept through their villages. Defenseless against measles, smallpox, and the common cold, entire villages were annihilated. For example, in the mid-1500s, 40,000 Indians living in southern Bahia were struck with smallpox; only 3,000 survived (Ribeiro 1995: 52).

Brazilian anthropologist Darcy Ribeiro (1995: 43) argues that whatever the immediate cause of death, many Indians actually "died of sadness"; stripped of their culture and denied their humanness, "they were certain that the only possible future would be a terrible negation of the past, a life not worthy to be lived by true people." Without the will to survive, they became easy victims to European germs and viruses.

In 1500, as many as five million Indians lived in the region that became modern Brazil, but only two million remained in 1700 and few along the coast (Ribeiro 1995). (Figure 3–1 shows the changes in the Brazilian population from 1500 to 1800.) Between **genocide** and flight, the coastal indigenous population was so devastated that the Portuguese turned to Africa to replace lost Indian labor. Despite the rapid annihilation of the coastal populations, bits of their cultures survive.

FIGURE 3–1

Brazilian Population, 1500–1800

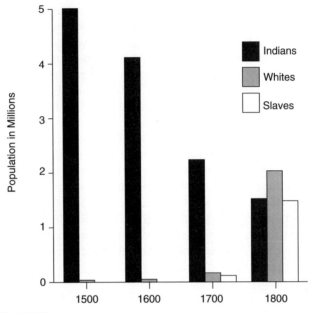

Source: Ribeiro (1995).

Practices that the Tupí-Guaraní taught the early Portuguese settlers—how to farm, hunt, and fish; how to use local materials to make cooking utensils and build houses—have been passed down generation after generation in rural Brazil. Though the Indian populations are gone, the Brazilian landscape carries names that evoke their spirits: Caruaru, Araraquara, Votuporanga. Even English was enriched, with words like *jaguar* and *hammock* now part of our everyday language.

Savanna Cultures

In the drier interior highlands were smaller populations of foraging groups such as the Gê and Bororó language groups (West 1993). Small, nomadic bands were scattered throughout the Brazilian plateau, inhabiting marginal areas unsuitable for the tribes of the tropical forest cultures. Relying on hunting and gathering for their survival, these bands required large territories in which to follow the migration of prey and to find a variety of plants during the cycle of seasons.

Isolated from the coast, the savanna cultures were not as quickly or severely affected by Portuguese colonization. By the time significant, regular contact did occur, the labor shortage had been addressed by the African slave trade. The savanna cultures, then, were viewed primarily as a hindrance to the exploitation of land and minerals that, from the European perspective, the Indians appeared to use so inefficiently. Thus, although the savanna bands were not needed for their labor, they met the same deadly fate as tribes of tropical forests.

Contemporary Situation
of the Indigenous Populations

By 1900, the original indigenous population of five million had fallen below one million and survivors occupied the most isolated regions. In the 20th century, as the Brazilian interior was opened to development, the pattern of conquest repeated itself. From 1900 to 1957, 80 tribes were exterminated by warfare and disease. By 1957, only 200,000 Indians remained in all of Brazil, one-twenty-fifth of the population at the time of European contact (Ribeiro 1995).

This genocide occurred despite the best efforts of a very remarkable Brazilian army officer, Candid Mariano da Silva Rondon. In 1890, Rondon was commissioned to lead an expedition into the interior of Brazil to map unexplored areas and make contact with the indigenous populations. Guided by the principle "die if necessary, but never kill," Rondon established contact with previously hostile tribes without a single Indian death, though some members of his own expedition were fatally wounded.

In 1910, Rondon successfully lobbied the government to establish the Indian Protection Service (SPI) to protect the indigenous populations from harmful contact by Brazilian society. Rondon hoped that the SPI would provide a buffer between Indians and Brazilians so that indigenous cultures could survive. The goal was to give Brazilian Indians the "right to be different . . . [the] right to be Indian" (Ribeiro 1995: 147). The Brazilian government committed itself to guarantee tribal lands so that surviving groups could maintain their cultural integrity.

The SPI was able to protect some tribes from the most harmful effects of contact with outsiders by giving them time to adapt. For example, the Kaingáng, contacted in 1912, became successful coffee farmers. Thus, a few tribes were integrated into Brazilian society without cultural disintegration. In most cases, though, the SPI lacked the resources to stop the invasion of tribal lands (Davis 1977). For example, 200,000 acres set aside as tribal lands in Rio Grande do Sul in 1913 were reduced to less than 80,000 acres by 1967 (Bodley 1990).

After Rondon's death (1958), SPI officials became tied to ranching interests, pacifying tribes so that *fazendeiros* could use their land. A 1968 government report documented SPI abuses, ranging from the use of dynamite, machine guns, and poison to massacre villages, to prostitution, slavery, and the illegal sale of Indian lands. As a result, one in five SPI employees was charged with crimes and the SPI itself was abolished, replaced with a new agency, the National Indian Foundation (FUNAI).

Little changed with the new name, as FUNAI appears more committed to integrating indigenous populations into Brazilian society than protecting them from exploitation and annihilation (Davis 1977; Bodley 1990). Unfortunately, when Indians are "integrated," it is as the poorest, least-skilled, and lowest-status workers, entering Brazilian society on the very bottom.

By 1993, less than 175,000 Indians remained in Brazil (IBGE 1995). This may be an underestimate—Wearne (1996) cites a figure of 325,000—but even the higher number means that just 0.2 percent of the population is indigenous. The only Tupí-Guaraní remnants living as they did in 1500 are in scattered villages deep in the Amazon rain forest. Tribes such as the Yanomamo are renowned, and feared, for their fierce defense of their isolation and autonomy. Even the vast Amazon, however, no longer protects the Yanomamo from encroachment; in September 1992, a village was massacred by gold miners in retaliation for an earlier conflict in which the Yanomamo had attempted to expel miners from their tribal lands (Maybury-Lewis 1997: 28).

Indians controlled 100 percent of the Brazilian territory in 1500 but now occupy about 16 percent, only half of which is officially demarcated and protected by law. Protected lands are not owned by the tribes but by the government, which grants the tribes the right of use. Thus, tribes are dependent on the state, legal "minors" whose "parent" is the state (Coelho 1996: 275).

Despite formidable forces arrayed against them, Brazil's Indians have become increasingly sophisticated in their struggles to defend their lands and cultures. Mario Juruna, a Xavante leader, became famous for tape-recording meetings with government officials to prevent them from breaking promises; in 1982, he was elected to the Brazilian Congress (Page 1995: 97–98). The Kayapó used video cameras to document illegal land invasions and forged an alliance with the British singer Sting to publicize their struggles. From 1982 to 1990, 48 organizations were created to defend Indian rights. As a result, in 1991–92 the government demarcated 36 million acres of protected tribal lands. The battle for survival remains in doubt, however, as the pressures to exploit their lands continue to mount (Wearne 1996: 172–73).

THE EUROPEAN CONTRIBUTION
The Portuguese

When Cabral landed on Brazil's coast in 1500, he represented a nation that was neither very old, very powerful, nor very large. The Iberian peninsula had experienced a succession of invasions, including the Iberians (1000 B.C.) for whom the region is named. By the fifth century, the inhabitants were Christians; but they were conquered in 711 by Muslim Moors from North Africa. The earldom of Portugal became the center of resistance to both

Moors and Castellans to the east. By 1250, the Portuguese had expelled the Moors and finally won independence from Castile in 1385.

As a small, new nation, Portugal was disadvantaged in the intra-European struggle for empire; but perched on the continent's extreme southwest corner, it was perfectly situated to pursue opportunities in the wider world. Thus, the Portuguese were in the forefront of the technological advances that made long-distance ocean travel in sailing ships possible. After exploring the west coast of Africa, Bartolomeu Dias was the first European to round the southern tip of Africa in 1488. Ten years later, Vasco da Gama opened the sea route to India (1497–99); a Portuguese navigator, Fernão de Magalhães (better known as Ferdinand Magellan because he sailed under the Spanish flag), was the first to sail completely around the globe (1519–21).

Exploration was costly, but the Portuguese believed that the discovery of Asian trade routes would amply reward them for their investment. In Asia were goods (spices and silk) in high demand in Europe and societies willing (or who could be forced) to trade for European goods. In Brazil, though, the Tupí-Guaraní produced nothing that Europe wanted, so the Portuguese replaced the founding of trading posts with the establishment of a colonial administration to oversee the production of goods for export to Europe (Burns 1993; Dantas 1991; Page 1995).

The experience of Moorish rule and the decades of exploring the African coast produced a unique combination of traits in the Portuguese colonists. They were independent and daring, especially in the pursuit of profit, but avoided physical labor whenever possible. Although officially intolerant of other religions, in practice they were extraordinarily open to integrating non-Christian beliefs and practices into their own version of popular Catholicism. And despite considering themselves superior because of their lighter skin, Portuguese males seemed to prefer darker-skinned women as sexual partners.

As a small nation with only one-fifth the population of Brazil's indigenous peoples and formed by the melding of numerous invading populations, the Portuguese did not see themselves primarily in racial terms. From the centuries-long struggle with Islam, the religious identity was central. Thus, the only requirement for entering Brazil was to be Catholic. As a result many "new Christians" (converted Jews), as well as other Europeans and even Middle Easterners, settled in Brazil. The expulsion of French Huguenots from Rio de Janeiro (1567) and the Dutch Calvinists from Pernambuco (1654) effectively eliminated the Protestant threat until the 19th century (Burns 1993).

Later European Immigration

Following abolition in 1888, the Brazilian elite deliberately promoted European immigration to replace the former slaves, believing that European laborers were innately superior—more intelligent and harder working. It was hoped that the *embranquicimento* (whitening) of the population by infusions of European blood would raise the cultural level of Brazil and speed modernization (Skidmore 1993).

From 1884 to 1957, 76 percent of all immigrants came from just three countries: Italy, Portugal, and Spain (Smith 1963). **Assimilation** was relatively easy as they came from Catholic cultures and spoke similar Romance languages. Distinct European ethnicities play a minimal role in Brazilian culture as within a generation or two most European immigrants became Brazilian. Assimilation was facilitated because being Portuguese is not high status despite their role as the original colonizers. In fact, the most common ethnic jokes in Brazil are told at their expense.

Immigration's impact was minimized because the total number of immigrants was small: only 4.8 million between 1884 and 1957, fewer than 65,000 annually (Smith 1963). In contrast, during roughly the same period (1890–1960) 26.4 million immigrants came to the United States (Applebaum and Chambliss 1995). The number of foreign-born in Brazil never exceeded 7 percent of the population and by 1980 had fallen to less than 1 percent (IBGE 1995).

The Portuguese Legacy

The Portuguese were always a minority, but as the colonial elite, they profoundly shaped Brazil's development. The major colonial institutions—the state, religion, the stratification system, family—remain strong today. The impact of these Portuguese legacies on modern Brazil are examined in the following chapters.

Beyond their political and economic contributions, the Portuguese helped define the Brazilian spirit. When contrasting their own culture with that of the United States, Brazilians quickly point out that English has no equivalent for the Portuguese concept of *saudade*—the intense emotion that comes with longing for something that is gone, perhaps forever. What sets this idea apart from anything in English is that this emotion embraces both deep sorrow and deep joy. It is good to feel the pain of *saudades* because it makes us human; it reflects the ability to love people or places enough to sorrow at their absence (Matta 1993).

> You cry without understanding that *saudade*
>   is much better than happiness
> because it is the happiness that remained!
> (Manuel Bandeira, quoted in Matta 1993: 34)

THE AFRICAN CONTRIBUTION

The first African slave ship arrived in 1538, but at first the flow of slaves was slow. By 1600, less than 50,000 slaves had entered Brazil; but as the sugar economy grew so did the demand for slaves. When the slave trade ended around 1870, 3.6 million Africans had been transported to Brazil (some estimates exceed 6 million). Brazil received 38 percent of the 9.6 million slaves brought to the western hemisphere; only 4 percent entered the United States (Lombardi, Lombardi, and Stoner 1983). Brazil has the largest African population outside of Africa itself.

In Brazil, slaves were recognized as belonging to three major **ethnic groups**. The preferred slaves were Sudanese, such as the Yoruba and Dahoman from west Africa between Liberia and Nigeria. Reputed to be amiable, hardworking, and intelligent, they were found throughout coastal Brazil. From farther north came the Guinea-Sudanese, who were concentrated in Bahia. Many were Muslim and literate in Arabic, whereas many of their Portuguese masters were unable to read or write (Freyre 1946). Skilled workers, they were responsible for many of the uprisings that plagued the colony. A large number of Bantu slaves from southern Africa, with a reputation for adaptability, were located in Rio and Minas Gerais. Thus, the Portuguese recognized cultural and ethnic diversity among Africans, even though it was perceived in terms of simplified **stereotypes**.

In 1700 there were 150,000 slaves, one for every European; by 1800 the slave population had multiplied 10 times to 1.5 million, or 30 percent of the total population (Ribeiro 1995: 151). Slave population growth was not caused by high fertility but by the constant importation of new slaves. More male slaves were imported than females, perhaps four times as many (Ribeiro 1995: 163). *Fazendeiros* found it cheaper to import new slaves than to pay the costs of lower productivity of pregnant field-workers and feeding and clothing children too young to work.

The constant stream of new arrivals allowed Brazilian slaves to maintain stronger ties to Africa than occurred in the United States, where the slave trade was abolished in 1808. Repeated infusions of African culture, language, and religion prevented complete assimilation. Thus, despite enormous obstacles, Africans maintained some cultural integrity, though there was a blending of the different cultures from which they came.

Slave Rebellions

Slaves drew on this cultural reservoir to sustain a series of rebellions (Degler 1971). Although direct attacks on the *fazendeiros* were always defeated (at times only with great difficulty), the most successful resistance was the creation of *quilombos*—communities of escaped slaves in isolated areas of the interior. The most famous *quilombo* was Palmares, a coalition of villages, whose existence defied the Portuguese for a hundred years. From small beginnings around 1597, Palmares grew to a population of approximately 20,000. It was viewed as such a threat that between 1672 and 1694 (when it was finally defeated) the Portuguese sent an average of one expedition every 15 months to attack Palmares (Dantas 1991: 74–75; Burns 1993: 47).

Children at a birthday party illustrate the race mixing that characterizes the Brazilian population.

Africanization of Brazilian Culture

African culture permeates Brazil but is greatest in the coastal regions of Pernambuco, Bahia, and Rio de Janeiro. In effect, Portuguese culture was Africanized to become Brazilian. Given the large number of slaves, their profound influence is understandable; it was the relatively few female slaves, though, who were the primary transmitters of African culture. As wet nurses, nannies, cooks, and maids, female slaves socialized the master's children (even the masters themselves) into the language, values, and lore of Africa. Their food was prepared by African cooks; bedtime songs and stories were African; the explanations for daily life—sickness, love, weather—were grounded in African knowledge of how the world worked. In effect, it was the slaves who taught the Portuguese master how to live in the Brazilian tropics, completing the education begun by the Tupí-Guaraní.

RACE MIXING: BECOMING BRAZILIAN

According to the 1991 census, 55 percent of the Brazilian population is white, 39 percent is brown, and only 5 percent is black (see Figure 3–2; Coelho 1996: 269). The majority report being white because they have European ancestors. Because being lighter is higher status, Brazilians often "round up" when classifying themselves (Twine 1998). In fact, most Brazilians are of mixed ancestry—every possible combination of

FIGURE 3–2

Brazilian Racial Mix (according to the national census), 1940–1991

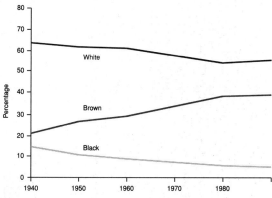

Source: Coelho (1996).

indigenous, European, and African. It is the union of the three racial and cultural groups that makes Brazil unique. In no other place in the world did such large populations of Asians (Indians), Europeans, and Africans intermix to such an extent.

Race mixing was caused by two major factors. First, the typical Portuguese colonist was a single male seeking his fortune in the New World, in sharp contrast with most North American settlers who came as family units. During the early years, then, when the cultural pattern of racial mixing was established, there were very few European women in Brazil. Despite appeals for female immigrants, in 1551 only three arrived, nine in 1553, and seven more in 1559, never enough to maintain a racially pure European population (Ribeiro 1995).

Second, although there was demographic pressure for Portuguese men to mate with Indian and African women, it also is clear that Portuguese men expressed few if any reservations about such intermixing. In fact, many Portuguese actually preferred Indian and African partners. Brazilian sociologist Gilberto Freyre (1946) argued that during the centuries of Moorish rule in Portugal, the racial hierarchy was inverted, with the lighter-skinned Portuguese serving the darker-skinned Moors. Thus, it was the Moorish women who were high status and unavailable to Portuguese men, who came to view dark skin as attractive. In contemporary Brazil, men frequently declare that the most beautiful women are the brown-skinned Brazilian *mulata*. This attraction is highly sexual, as lighter-skinned women are preferred for marriage because they are generally of a higher social and economic status. A popular folk saying explicitly expresses this attitude: "a white woman for marriage, a black woman to cook, a *mulata* for sex."

Beneath the physical attraction is a strong undercurrent of racist and sexist stereotyping in which darker-skinned women are viewed primarily as sexual objects. Because slave owners assumed that they possessed the right of sexual access to their Indian and African property, much of the early race mixing was violent. Freyre (1946: 255) wrote approvingly about the *"mulatto* girl . . . [w]ho initiated us[!] into physical love and . . . gave us our first complete sensation of being a man"; not until 100 pages later does he acknowledge that "it was not a request but a command to which she had to accede" (349). The belief that dark-skinned women have no right to say no to light-skinned, especially wealthy, men continues to rear its ugly head in contemporary relations between Brazilian men and their maids (*Sindicato dos Trabalhadores Domésticos* 1996).

RACIAL INEQUALITIES

In Brazil, one's **life chances** (the likelihood that an individual will have access to scarce resources during his or her life) are severely constrained by skin color. In 1988, to commemorate the 100th anniversary of the emancipation of Brazilian slaves, the news magazine *Veja* reported on the status of the descendants of the freed slaves:

> The person born black has a 30 percent greater chance of dying before the age of 5 than the one born white. Growing up, she is twice as likely (as a white) to drop out of school without learning to read or write. When she dies, she comes to the end of a life that when she was born had an expectancy of only 50 years. If she had been white, her life expectancy would have been 63 years (quoted in Coelho 1996: 277).

The magazine went on to state that "out of every ten Brazilians, four are black, but out of every ten poor Brazilians six are black" (quoted in Page 1995: 60). Only 19 percent of whites earn less than the minimum wage, compared to almost 75 percent of those defined as black or brown (Margolis 1992).

One reason blacks are more likely to be poor is that they are less integrated into the educational system, with illiteracy rates almost twice as high as for whites—40 percent compared to 22 percent (Margolis 1992). The further one goes in the educational system, the worse the inequality becomes, even after controlling for parents' education and household income (Lovell and Wood 1998). White Brazilians are 8.5 times more likely to enter university than blacks and 5 times more likely than brown Brazilians. In the United States, the comparable figure is 1.4 times more likely (Silva and Hasenbalg 1992). Black Brazilians also are less rewarded for the education that they do receive: "whites earn 3.5 percent more for each additional year of schooling, while *pardos* [browns] earn 2.3 percent and blacks 2.2 percent" (Margolis 1992: 7). Even in the same job, blacks earn less than whites. This is true in every occupation from doctors (22 percent less) to bricklayers (11 percent less) to school teachers (18 percent less) (Page 1995: 59).

HIDDEN RACISM

Surprisingly few dark-skinned Brazilians identify this kind of **institutional discrimination,** in which structural barriers block access to scarce resources, as racism. Brazilians often conceptualize racism in legal terms; and because there are no legal barriers to access resources—such as existed in South African apartheid or in the Jim Crow laws in the United States—then by definition there is no racial discrimination. Brazilians also think of racism as expressed in interpersonal relations, when someone directly and overtly discriminates on the basis of race. This kind of discrimination, however, is usually interpreted as a personal problem of racist individuals rather than as a social problem requiring fundamental changes in Brazilian culture and institutions.

Despite the discrimination, prejudice, and institutional racism, Brazilians of all colors generally interact with so little of the tension common in the United States that it has been referred to as *racismo cordial,* "polite racism" (Twine 1998: 75). One reason is that because race is a continuum, there are no sharp distinctions; prejudice and discrimination are not either/or, but more or less. Thus, Brazil does not have a legacy of legal race discrimination; even during slavery, emancipated slaves faced no legal restrictions based on race (Degler 1971). In fact, legal discrimination was impractical as it would have required an almost infinite number of drinking fountains, bathrooms, residential areas, and so forth to separate all the races.

A second reason for the lack of recognition of racism is that most blacks are also poor and economic discrimination is much more apparent and harsh. No Brazilian would be so naive as to claim that their country is an economic democracy. Brazil is a highly stratified class society with some of the world's greatest economic inequality. For poor black Brazilians, the disadvantage of being poor is felt much more directly than is the disadvantage of race. This perception is reinforced by the fact that poor whites and poor blacks live together in the same communities. Blacks' poor white neighbors are also disadvantaged by class, seeming to negate the racial advantage of whiteness (Burdick 1998; Twine 1998). Thus, the place in Brazil where racial democracy may come closest to reality is among the most economically disadvantaged.

Finally, Brazilians of all colors are comfortable in interracial social interaction because many have done so from birth within the home. Because of the long history of intermarriage and the size of kin networks, many families include a wide range of racial appearance. While attending the birthday celebration of a good friend's daughter, I was amazed at the racial diversity of the **extended family.** I could think of no time in the United States when I was in a similarly diverse group of people who were so intimate with one another. Especially striking was that in Brazil it seemed so completely normal.

RACE-BASED MOVEMENTS

There has never been a Brazilian equivalent of the civil rights movement in the United States, a national grassroots movement dedicated to the elimination of racial discrimination (Hanchard 1994; Burdick 1998). Part of the reason is that discrimination in Brazil is much more subtle and ambiguous than in the United States. But even if the discrimination were recognized, mobilization would be difficult because it is not clear who the potential members of such a **social movement** would be. Only 5 percent of the population claims to be black. For most Brazilians with African ancestry, there appears to be more to be gained by deemphasizing this fact than by drawing attention to it (Burdick 1998).

Despite the difficulties, however, a beginning has been made to redress the most blatant forms of discrimination. The United Movement against Racial Discrimination (MNUCDR) was established in 1978 to increase awareness of racism and to engage in political activism. In 1988, Brazilians celebrated the 100th anniversary of slavery's abolition and rewrote the federal constitution. The coincidence of events created enough pressure to include a clause in the constitution that for the very first time makes racial discrimination a "jailable offense" (Margolis 1992: 6).

At the cultural level, Afro-Brazilians increasingly have turned to Africa and the Afro-populations of the Caribbean and North America to renew their cultural traditions. African music, religion, and dress have all regained popularity in Brazil. Political movements like the MNUCDR have mainly attracted the middle class and intellectuals; but these cultural movements have attracted poor Brazilians, increasing their awareness of and pride in their heritage (Margolis 1992). Nonblack Brazilians are enriched by the encounter with African culture, but they also are confronted with the fact that their own Brazilian culture is inconceivable without this African influence.

CONCLUSION

Race in Brazil is a continuum ranging from high-status whites to low-status blacks; in between are an amazing number of recognized gradations. The concept of race is further complicated by (1) appearance, including hair, mouth, eyes, and so forth; (2) economic status, with wealthier individuals considered lighter; and (3) social distance, the more friendly the relationship the lighter.

This racial continuum originated from the violent encounter of three groups: indigenous peoples, Europeans, and Africans. Most Brazilians are of mixed descent, reflecting in infinite combinations the physical traits of all three groups. This race mixing is used as evidence to claim that Brazil is a racial democracy. Brazil can be justifiably proud of the relative ease of interaction between Brazilians of all colors, but significant racial discrimination exists. Blacks are more likely to be poor, less likely to finish school, and more likely to be unemployed.

Brazil has never experienced a major social movement confronting racial inequality. One of the principle reasons is that because there are no sharp racial categories, there is no sharp division between privileged and disadvantaged groups. Discrimination is rarely overt in Brazil; instead, it subtly reflects the fine gradations of racial categories, making its elimination extremely difficult. Brazilians of all colors, however, are increasingly aware and proud of their African heritage. Many of the most valued elements of Brazilian culture—music, dance, religion—have their origins in Africa and have become Brazilian through their incorporation of indigenous and European influences.

CHAPTER 4

The Brazilian Economy

On October 27, 1945, a little boy named Luis Ignácio da Silva was born into a poor peasant family in the dry, rural backlands of northeast Brazil. His father—who would not meet Luis until five years later—had left to find work in the industrial megacity of São Paulo, 2,000 miles away. When he was seven, Luis traveled with his family for 13 days in the back of an open truck to join his father. Like other poor Brazilian children, Luis worked hard—cutting wood, carrying water, selling peanuts and tapioca in the streets. Eventually, at age 14, Luis found employment in one of the many factories springing up in the city to supply the expanding automobile industry (Morel 1989).

Millions of Brazilians lived similar stories of migration, employment, and unemployment, of hardship and, if not success, at least economic survival. Luis isn't one of these anonymous millions because as an adult he became "Lula"—a union leader, arrested, tortured, active in the opposition that toppled the military regime, and twice nearly elected president of Brazil. While that political story will be told in the next chapter, this chapter analyzes the economic structures and processes that first produced Luis and later transformed him into Lula.

CONTRADICTIONS, CHANGE, CONTINUITY

One common image is of Brazil as a gigantic tropical plantation growing exotic export crops like mangos, rubber, and *cacão*. It's true that Brazil does export millions of dollars, worth of agricultural products, but this is only a small part of the economy. Currently, about 75 percent of all Brazilian exports are industrial goods; only 9 percent of the goods and services produced in Brazil come from agriculture or mining, while 34 percent are manufactured goods (Coelho 1996: 43, 172).

The Brazilian economy is much more complex than is implied by the stereotype of the tropical plantation. It is the world's tenth largest economy, exporting televisions, cars, even military aircraft. Brazil's computer industry produces both hardware and software. But Brazil is also a country with a 1-800 number to report violations of the antislavery law and where millions of children live on city streets or labor in sugar fields.

Complexity and rapid development sometimes obscure the fact that there are at least three major continuities in the Brazilian economy. The first continuity is inequality. In the 1980s, the World Bank identified Brazil as having the greatest inequality in the world. Although some countries are richer and some are poorer, in no country is the gap between rich and poor greater. This inequality has grown worse over the last few decades, but it has plagued Brazil since colonial times.

The second continuity is instability, specifically the repetition of cycles of **boom and bust.** At different points in time, Brazil has depended heavily on a single product for economic growth. Early on, sugar was the principle product, but later gold, rubber, and coffee took turns driving the economy. Reliance on a single **primary product,** however, is risky because when demand ebbs and prices drop, the entire economy falls with it. Perhaps the most poignant symbol of these boom-and-bust cycles is the magnificent opera house built in Manaus in the heart of the Amazon during the turn-of-the-century rubber boom. With its elegant gold leaf and imported Italian marble, construction cost $2 million in 1896 (Burns 1993: 289). But when the demand for Brazilian rubber fell, the opera house was abandoned. For many years, until it was reopened in 1990, the only music heard within its vacant shell was the songs of birds nesting in the rafters. Economic diversification accompanying industrialization finally may be reducing Brazil's chronic economic instability.

The third continuity is Brazil's dependence on the international market (Furtado 1963). Brazil relies heavily on exports because so many people are so poor that the local market is too small to sustain economic growth. Brazil also relies heavily on foreign capital (investments and loans) as well as imported technology. Although foreign capital and technology accelerated industrialization, there was a cost. When interest rates rose during the late 1980s, Brazil was unable to pay off its loans and was forced to cut social service programs in order to get new loans to pay off the old. The costs and benefits of this external **dependence** have been the focus of continual conflict throughout Brazilian history (Cardoso and Faletto 1979).

The three continuities of inequality, instability, and dependence are tightly interlinked. Low wages keep Brazilian exports competitive in the international market, but this maintains the high level of inequality. Widespread poverty limits the size of the internal market because little income means little purchasing power. Because the local market is relatively small, the economy is vulnerable to price fluctuations in the international market. These interconnections mean that there are no simple solutions to Brazil's economic problems.

MODERNIZATION OR DEPENDENCY?

Although there are significant continuities, the Brazilian economy certainly is not the same as it was in 1500 or even 1900. Brazil is an industrial giant, with production more diversified than at any time in its history. How are we to understand this mixture of continuity and change? The two theories introduced in Chapter 1 offer different answers. Modernization theory emphasizes the transformations of the Brazilian economy, arguing that industrialization, urbanization, and rising levels of education and life expectancy are all evidence that Brazil is becoming modern (Schneider 1996). The dependency theory claims that the fundamental problems of the colonial economy may have mutated, but they have not gone away. Brazil is no longer dependent on a few agricultural products like sugar and coffee, but it remains dependent on foreign markets and foreign sources of capital (Evans 1979).

Because there have been both change and continuity, the evidence for each theory is mixed and sociologists disagree on how to interpret the data (Firebaugh and Beck 1994; Dixon and Boswell 1996). This is more than just an academic debate. The interpretation of Brazil's economic problems shapes the choice of possible solutions. Is foreign investment the cure or the disease? Will continued industrialization significantly reduce poverty or will it simply move poverty from the countryside to the city?

THE PRECOLONIAL ECONOMY

Before the arrival of the Portuguese, the inhabitants of Brazil were primarily foragers and horticulturalists. **Foraging societies** find food by hunting for meat and gathering plants, roots, and fruits. **Horticultural societies** produce food by clearing garden plots with slash-and-burn technology. Horticulturalists may forage to supplement their food production.

Despite different economic strategies, the precolonial foraging and horticultural populations in Brazil shared important characteristics. First, both strategies are highly efficient in the use of labor. The indigenous populations produced everything that they needed to survive working far fewer than 40 hours a week. These cultures were not wealthy in material goods, but there was abundant time to create cultures rich in religion, art, and leisure. Second, neither economic strategy used land permanently. Foragers follow the movement of animals and plant cycles; horticulturalists move every few years to maintain the fertility of their garden plots. Third, because both economic strategies used land nonintensively, population density was relatively low; in 1500 the indigenous population was far less than the current population of the city of Rio de Janeiro.

THE COLONIAL ECONOMY

The Portuguese colonized Brazil because they expected to make a profit. The foraging and horticultural societies they encountered along the Atlantic coast, however, weren't producing goods that could be resold in Europe, like Asian spices and silk. The Portuguese, however, discovered a tree that yielded a profitable red dye, which provided the economic basis to continue the search for other exploitable resources. The commercial motivation for exploration is underscored by the fact that the name adopted for the Portuguese colony came from that first export—brazilwood.

Exploitation of brazilwood proceeded erratically. The Portuguese were not interested in performing the hard labor of cutting trees and transporting them to ships waiting along the coast, so they attempted to enlist the indigenous population in the work. Except in exchange for some Portuguese item that struck their fancy, however, Indians saw little reason to work so hard when all their basic needs were already met. Attempts to force them to work were resisted by flight or war.

To set the colony on a more orderly and profitable foundation, in 1534 King João III began dividing the colony into 15 captaincies, which were distributed to donees responsible for developing their territory. These captaincies were quite large, as they averaged 150 miles wide (north-south) and extended westward from the Atlantic Ocean to the line of Tordesillas somewhere in the continent's uncharted interior. The most successful captaincy was Pernambuco under the administration of Duarte Coelho. Determined to provide profitable exports to Europe, Coelho ordered the planting of sugarcane, tobacco, and cotton. Sugar quickly became the most important crop, with sugar mills springing up to fill the ships headed back to Europe (Dantas 1991: 27–29; Burns 1993: 27–28).

The Coelho family became the richest in Brazil if not in the entire Portuguese empire. Over 450 years later, the Coelhos remain wealthy and powerful. At one point in the early 1980s, my wife and I traveled to Petrolina in the western *sertão* of Pernambuco, the home of Nilo Coelho, a powerful federal senator. One night a group of men stayed up late drinking and playing loud music outside our hotel room, making it impossible for my wife, who was pregnant, and myself to sleep. I went down to the hotel desk and asked the manager to tell the men to lower the volume. In horror, the manager said, "Do you know who that is?" I obviously didn't. It was Nilo Coelho's nephew, and there was no way the manager was going to tell him to do anything. Instead, we were given a nicer room on the other side of the hotel; everyone was happy and no one got hurt.

If anyone could be considered the father of Brazil, it would be Duarte Coelho. Not only did he establish the financial viability of the colony, but the economic structures he initiated persist as the basis of the modern Brazilian economy. The three continuities identified at the beginning of this chapter all originated under Duarte Coelho's leadership. Inequality was established in two ways. First, land, the primary source of wealth, was concentrated in a few hands. This is in stark contrast to the United States, where there was a concerted effort to make land widely available, at least to all white males. Second, the use of coerced labor, Indian and then African, ensured the emergence of stark hierarchical class divisions.

The cycle of boom and bust originated with the concentration on sugar production. The green hills of Pernambuco's coast still are covered for mile after mile with a single crop—sugarcane. It's almost unbelievable, but these fields have been planted with the same crop for four and a half centuries. Only the incredible fertility of the soil could sustain this monocrop system for so long. Reliance on sugar, though, meant that the economy mirrored the fluctuating price of a single product. After 1650, other regions began producing sugar (the Caribbean, south and southeast Asia) and the Brazilian sugar industry declined. Between 1650 and 1715, income from sugar fell by two-thirds and the economy of the northeast stagnated (Burns 1993).

Sugar was also the origin of Brazil's foreign dependence, as the European market was the very reason that sugarcane was planted. Virtually Europe's only source of sugar for 100 years, the *fazendeiros* reaped huge profits. Approximately 97 percent of the income from sugar sales went to mill and plantation owners; the other 3 percent went primarily to feed and clothe slaves. The owners had little incentive to invest in diversifying or increasing the efficiency of production. The establishment of factories in Brazil was illegal (to protect Portuguese producers), and the guaranteed European market meant that there was little incentive to improve production techniques. Thus, owners spent their enormous profits on conspicuous consumption and the importation of European luxury goods like the French wines mentioned in Chapter 2 (Hewlett 1980).

By the time the ban on Brazilian manufacturing was lifted (1821), the damage already had been done. The industrial revolution was in full swing in Europe, and local attempts to industrialize were frustrated by the inability to compete with European factories producing manufactured goods more cheaply and of higher quality. By 1821, the sugar boom was over; the massive profits of the early monopoly years had been dissipated unproductively, and little capital remained for investment in manufacturing.

After sugar, other primary products took turns leading the Brazilian economy. Gold was discovered in 1695, and during the next 100 years Brazil produced an estimated 80 percent of the world's gold, nearly 2 million pounds worth $10.4 trillion at a 1997 price of $325 an ounce. The Portuguese crown claimed 20 percent of all the gold and then imposed additional taxes (e.g., per slave used in gold mining) to take an even larger cut.

As with sugar, much of the gold profit that remained in Brazil was spent in nonproductive ways. England was the greatest beneficiary because the gold flooding Portugal was used to purchase British manufactured goods. Thus, Brazilian gold fueled England's industrial revolution, but it produced few long-term benefits in either Brazil or Portugal (Furtado 1963; Burns 1993: 67).

As gold production declined over the second half of the 18th century, sugar reclaimed its position as the leading export. During the 1820s, sugar exports represented 30 percent of the total and cotton was second at 21 percent. By the 1830s, however, coffee was the new export king with 44 percent. Coffee's importance increased through the second half of the 19th century and the first three decades of the 20th century. By the 1920s, coffee represented nearly 75 percent of all Brazilian exports.

Introduced into Pará in 1737, coffee was first planted in Rio de Janeiro in 1776, where it quickly took root. From Rio, coffee spread southward into the state of São Paulo, which soon became the center of coffee production (Dantas 1991: 132–33, 197). At the turn of the century, Brazil was producing 75 to 80 percent of all the coffee in the world; São Paulo alone was responsible for approximately half of the world's coffee (Burns 1993: 263).

The coffee boom, however, also ended in a bust. In 1929, the American stock market crashed and the effects rippled around the globe, causing a worldwide depression. Brazil was hit quickly and hard because half of its coffee exports went to the United States. With 26 million sacks of unwanted coffee beans stockpiled in São Paulo in 1930, more than the entire world consumed in 1929, the price plummeted from 22.5¢ per pound to just 8¢ (Burns 1993: 344). Without the revenues from coffee exports, Brazil was forced to cut back the importation of manufactured goods. Total imports dropped from $US 417 million in 1929 to just $US 108 million two years later (Baer 1983: 43). Once again, the Brazilian economy was devastated by reliance on a single export.

INDUSTRIALIZATION: 1930–1964

Apparent disaster, however, proved to be an opportunity. The Great Depression was so severe that Brazil's reliance on the export sector was effectively (if temporarily) broken. Unable to sell its primary products (coffee, sugar, and rubber) or to buy European and North American manufactured goods, Brazil's leaders had to choose between continuing traditional economic policies and being prepared to endure stagnation until the world economy improved or for the first time in its history embark on a serious program of industrialization.

The government opted for industrialization, implementing four major policies: (1) The government bought the stockpiled coffee to keep the coffee planters from going bankrupt. (2) The government offered incentives to invest the coffee payments in industry. Given that agriculture was no longer profitable, tax breaks and tariffs on imported goods were effective in attracting capital for local industry. (3) The government itself invested in industrial sectors where there was insufficient private capital to generate new industry. State industries in "railroads, shipping, public utilities, and basic industrial goods" played a critical role in supporting private industry (Hewlett 1980: 38). (4) The government stimulated the emergence of an urban working and middle class to consume locally produced manufactured goods. Without a significant expansion of income, local demand would be insufficient to sustain local industry. Thus, the government became involved in wage policy, for the first time legalizing unions, establishing a minimum wage, and legislating workers' benefits.

The results were remarkable. In 1933, Brazilian industry broke all-time production records, while the United States remained locked in the depths of the depression. By 1939, textile production was 147 times greater than in 1929 and the output of metal products and paper had multiplied by factors of 3 and 7 respectively. Steel and cement production rose to meet the construction demands of industrialization. Total industrial output expanded more in the 10 years following the crash than in all previous Brazilian history (Baer 1983: 34–45).

Over the next several decades, Brazil continued its policy of **import substitution industrialization (ISI),** replacing manufactured imports, primarily mass consumer goods like clothing and housewares, with local production. Brazil was so successful that by 1961 only 1.5 percent of imports were manufactured consumer goods (Baer 1983: 60). In the decade following the crash, 318,000 manufacturing jobs were created, an increase of 24 percent; by 1960, industrial employment had more than doubled (UN-ECLA 1966: 13). The increasing importance of industry between 1930 and 1960, rising from 12 to 26 percent of the **gross domestic product (GDP),** mirrored a decline in Brazil's historical dependence on agriculture, falling from 24 to 13 percent of GDP (see Figure 4–1; SALA 1987).

The statistics summarize the magnitude of the changes that took place in Brazil, but numbers sometimes conceal the human drama. One of the millions of Brazilians who heard of the rapid industrialization occurring in the city of São Paulo was the father of Lula, the boy introduced at the beginning of the chapter. Lula's father joined the exodus, seeking work and a better life. Lula and his family soon followed. There were no guarantees, however, that their hopes would be fulfilled. Lula eventually found work in the burgeoning automobile industry, but not everyone was so fortunate. Millions of migrants ended up in *favelas*, barely surviving by doing odd jobs and domestic service (maids, cooks). Things were hard when seven-year-old Lula arrived in São Paulo in 1962, but little did he or other migrants know that the Brazilian economy was headed for a major crisis.

INDUSTRIALIZATION: THE 1960s AND 1970s

After three decades of rapid economic growth Brazil seemed on the verge of realizing its vast economic potential. But in the early 1960s, the

FIGURE 4–1

Transformation of the Brazilian Economy, 1920–1993

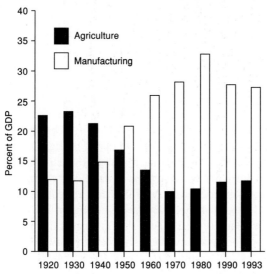

Source: SALA (1996).

economy ran into serious problems. The first sign of trouble was an ominous inflation rate of 29 percent in 1960, which accelerated to 73 percent in 1963 and in 1964 broke the 100 percent barrier (Kahil 1973; Torloni 1977). Inflation was a symptom of deeper problems. Ironically, the basic problem was that ISI had succeeded; local industry had almost completely replaced imports of manufactured consumer goods. Demand, however, was limited by Brazil's highly unequal income distribution. Boosting demand for manufactured consumer goods to keep ISI going required redistributing income downward to expand the local market—a politically popular move with workers, but highly unpopular with the politically powerful elite. Increasing exports would be no easier; high tariffs on imports facilitated industrialization but hadn't required attaining the efficiency needed to compete in international markets.

The intense political conflicts that erupted from this impasse provoked a military overthrow of the democratic government (discussed in the following chapter). The military regime decided against pursuing continued ISI growth. Instead, the regime pursued growth based on **deepening** industrialization, or **capital goods industrialization,** shifting emphasis from mass consumer goods to more expensive consumer durables, like cars and airplanes, and capital goods (machinery, chemicals, plastics) used to produce consumer goods.

A strategy of deepening, however, raised a new problem: how to pay for it. The technological requirements for industries like petrochemicals and aircraft were more complex and therefore more expensive than for ISI industries. More investment capital had to be found. One primary source was from **transnational corporations (TNCs).** Legal barriers to protect local capitalists were removed to facilitate the entrance of foreign investment. U.S. investment in manufacturing (the primary source) jumped from $723 million in 1965 to $6.9 billion just 20 years later (SALA 1988). The influx of foreign capital meant that while ISI industries like clothing, shoes, and paper remained locally controlled, the new, technologically advanced industries like chemicals, electronics, and transportation equipment were dominated by the TNCs (Evans 1979).

The second major source of capital was international loans to the Brazilian government. In 1966, external public debt stood at $3.2 billion; 20 years later, the Brazilian government owed foreign lenders $88.3 billion (SALA 1987, 1989). With billions of dollars at its disposal, state investment in industry and infrastructure (roads, hydroelectric dams, and so forth to support industry) skyrocketed. A 1981 study revealed that nearly 50 percent of the total assets of the 8,068 largest firms in Brazil were owned by state enterprises (Baer 1983: 213). Of the 30 largest firms (by sales) in 1984, 11 were state-owned, with average sales and profits nearly double those of private firms, either local or TNC (*Veja* 1986: 124–25).

The third crucial source of capital was Brazilian workers. During ISI, the government raised workers' wages to increase demand for mass consumer goods. From the late 1940s through the early 1960s, the real value of the minimum wage had risen steadily (see Figure 4–2). The economic elite, not workers, however, were the primary market for consumer durable and capital goods. Thus, economic policy was modified to redistribute income upward. As a result, the real value of the minimum wage fell by 30 percent between 1965 and 1976 (Flynn 1978: 161, 197; SALA 1984).

As a metalworker, Lula was one of the millions impacted by falling wages. Because the drop was caused by government policies, the experience radicalized Lula and many of his coworkers. By the 1970s, the declining standard of living provoked angry resistance from Brazilian workers, but in the short term the capital generated by low wages, combined with foreign investment and loans, provided a massive infusion of capital into the Brazilian economy, igniting such rapid growth that it was called the Brazilian "economic miracle." From 1968 to 1973, the economy grew at an average annual rate (controlling for inflation) of 11.5 percent. The economy slowed slightly in 1973–80 but continued expanding at a healthy yearly average of 7.1 percent (Alves 1985: 107). In comparison, economists are pleased when the United States economy grows 2–3 percent per year.

With the abandonment of ISI, dependence on exports returned. The percentage of GDP generated by trade almost doubled between 1970 (16 percent) and 1980 (30 percent). In 1970, the total value of Brazil's merchandise exports was just $2.8 billion; 15 years later it reached $25.6 billion. Expanding exports were driven by sales of manufactured goods,

FIGURE 4–2

Evolution of Real Minimum Wage in Brazil (1960 = 100), 1950–1976

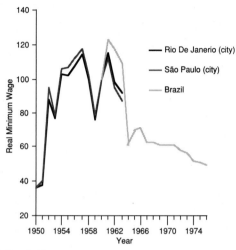

Source: Flynn (1978); Alves (1985).

which between 1970 and 1983 jumped from just 36 percent of exports to 74 percent; during the same period the percentage of agricultural exports fell from 54 percent to 18 percent (SALA 1989; Schneider 1996: 162).

Export dependence intensified, but Brazil had reduced the vulnerability of relying on one primary export product. As recently as 1955, 61 percent of Brazil's export earnings came from coffee alone; 30 years later, the leading agricultural export was soybeans at only 9.9 percent. Brazil also reduced its trade dependence on the United States. During the late 1960s, approximately one-third of Brazil's exports were sold to the United States, but by the early 1980s, the United States only purchased about one-fifth percent of Brazil's exports (SALA 1989).

THE LOST DECADE: THE 1980s

By the beginning of the 1980s, Brazil had a diverse, industrial economy that appeared on its way to solving some of the economic problems of its colonial heritage. In 1981, though, the economy crashed once again, revealing that although significant transformations had occurred, fundamental problems remained. A worldwide recession halted export expansion in its tracks. After growing by an average of 22.5 percent from 1970 to 1981, the value of Brazil's exports plummeted 13.3 percent in 1981–82 and had a negative average growth rate of 0.2 percent from 1981 to 1986 (SALA 1987; Schneider 1996: 162).

As international demand for Brazilian exports dwindled, the economic miracle died. In fact, the economy was so stagnant during the 1980s that it is known as the "lost decade." Trade dependence was not the only problem. International demand revived in the second half of the decade, but debt dependence hindered economic recovery. Foreign loans contracted with floating interest rates had to be repaid in hard currency (dollars, yen, deutsche marks) that could be acquired only through trade. During the 1960s and early 1970s, when interest rates were low and trade generated the profits to pay off the loans, even massive debt seemed unproblematic. As exports fell so did Brazil's ability to pay. In 1978, Brazil's debt service (required payments on the debt) was only 24.5 percent of its export earnings; by 1982, it had more than doubled to 57.1 percent. This meant that 57 percent of all the earnings from all the country's exports were required to pay the debt service. Although 1982 was the worst year, the ratio averaged more than 40 percent over the next four years.

The problem was worse than simply reduced revenues to pay off the debt. As the world economy settled into recession, inflation drove up interest rates. Thus, every time interest rates were adjusted upward, the cost of loans negotiated years earlier increased. Rising interest rates cost Brazil almost $35 billion from 1973 to 1986. Unable to pay off its old debt, Brazil was forced to seek new loans. From 1982 to 1986, Brazil's total foreign debt increased almost 50 percent, surpassing $110 billion. An estimated two-thirds of these new loans provided no new investment but were used to pay the interest on old debt (Roddick 1988: 128–33).

New debt was extremely costly. To acquire new loans from the International Monetary Fund (IMF), Brazil had to accept conditions that included policies designed to decrease local consumption to free more money for loan repayment. Suppressing wages reduced local consumption and freed more goods for export; cutting government benefits and services (education, health, pensions, food subsidies) saved money to pay the banks. The IMF referred to the conditions as an "adjustment program," but in Brazil and elsewhere they were commonly known as "austerity packages." In essence, the IMF required Brazilians to lower their standard of living to pay off the loans. This might seem fair; people should pay their debts. Yet countries are not individuals, and the ones who took out the loans were not the same ones required to make repayment. Most of the debt had been incurred by officials of the military dictatorship (1964–85) who, when the economy crashed, returned the government to civilians. Not all civilians, however, were asked to bear an equal share of the debt burden. The poor, who least benefited from the loans, were forced to tighten their belts to pay back the foreign banks (Kuczynski 1988; Roddick 1988).

During the 1980s, the quality of life for Brazil's poor steadily worsened. According to government standards, 65 hours of minimum wage work in 1965 were required to purchase a minimum food basket, but 115 hours were required in 1986 to purchase the same amount of food. The incidences of underweight newborns, anemia, and malnutrition all rose. Of 100 children, only 74 even started school and only 12 actually completed the primary grades (Roddick 1988: 143–44). Public hospitals, devastated by budget cuts, lacked staff, medicines, and even beds. A friend of mine from Caranguejo experienced severe hemorrhaging. Unable to afford private care, she was taken to a government hospital where there was no bed for her. She stayed up all night sitting in a chair until a mattress was brought to the hospital so she could at least lie on the floor.

Brazil's foreign debt remained among the largest in the world through the 1980s, but expanding exports helped Brazil weather the worst of the crisis. Inflation, however, returned with a vengeance, reaching record monthly highs of 30 to 40 percent. Prices rose so fast that they often changed daily. Every few years, the Brazilian currency was replaced in order to knock a few decimals off the prices of goods. In response, Brazilians developed creative methods of surviving. High inflation meant that money constantly lost its value, so saving it was worse than useless. Upon receiving their wages, Brazilians immediately bought whatever they needed for the coming weeks. If there was money left over, the rule was spend it or lose it. One trick was to buy unneeded items (televisions, stereos, and so forth) that could be resold later. Ironically, consumption became a form of savings.

CONTINUITY AND CHANGE: THE 1990s

During the 1990s, the Brazilian economy appeared more stable than it had in decades. Inflation finally was tamed, dropping to less than 10 percent a year. Demand for Brazil's increasingly diversified exports remained high. Brazil had a large industrial sector that was increasingly capable of developing high-tech products like computers and military aircraft.

Inequality

Yet, many of Brazil's basic economic problems persist. Despite decades of industrialization and economic growth, inequality has gotten worse. In 1960, the poorest 50 percent of all Brazilians received 17.4 percent of the national income; 10 years later, this had fallen to 14.9 percent. In the following two decades, the gap between rich and poor continued to grow. In 1990, the poorest 50 percent received only 11.2 percent of national income, a drop of over 35 percent in 30 years. In contrast, the richest 10 percent captured 49.7 percent of the total national income (Coelho 1996: 32).

The reality of this poverty, however, is not adequately expressed with numbers. For millions of Brazilians, poverty is the gnawing hunger that wakes them in the morning and accompanies them to bed at night. Worse than the hunger itself is the fear that precedes it: The fear that there will be no food for you and your children, the fear of not knowing when or if the hunger will end. In 1960, Carolina Maria de Jesus, a mother of three, published her diary of life in a São Paulo *favela*. In the entry for May 20, 1958, she wrote:

> How horrible it is to see a child eat and ask: "Is there more?" The word "more" keeps ringing in the mother's head as she looks in the pot and doesn't have any more. . . When I arrived from the [government] Palace that is in the city, my children ran to tell me that they had found some macaroni in the garbage. As the food supply was low I cooked some of the macaroni with beans. And my son João: "Uh huh. You told me that we weren't going to eat any more things from the garbage." It was the first time that I had failed to keep my word (1962: 40).

Even the hardest-working poor have no security that they will be able to feed their families. Gilson, one of my neighbors in Caranguejo, was trained to do body work on cars. Unemployed and desperate, he finally found a body shop that would take him on if he would work without pay for one month to prove himself. So he worked for free and at the end of the month he was told that his services were no longer needed. About this time, his wife gave birth and my wife went to see her. Graçinha was lying in bed with her baby born a few hours earlier; the other children were playing on the floor. There was not a single bean or grain of rice in the house. Gilson had left early that morning to look for work, but with no guarantees that even if he found work that he would be paid so he could bring home some food.

Land Concentration

This is the face of poverty, a face that needn't exist. Brazil has a land area larger than the continental United States, but it has less than 60 percent of the U.S. population. Brazil easily could produce enough food to eradicate hunger among its citizens. It fails to do so for two reasons: Land continues to be highly concentrated, and exporting produces greater profits than producing food for the local market.

Brazil has one of the world's most highly concentrated systems of landownership. Only 1 percent of landowners own 44 percent of all the farmland in holdings of 1,000 hectares (2,471 acres) or more. Thus, 58,000 landowners own nearly 165 million hectares, an average farm of over 7,000 acres. On the other hand, 53 percent of Brazilian farmers work less than 3 percent of the farmland on holdings of less than 10 hectares (24.7 acres). Most vulnerable are the estimated 13 million *sem terras* who own no land at all. About 6 million *sem terras* live on other people's land as renters, squatters, and sharecroppers; the rest are migrant day-laborers. More than 5 million of these rural workers earn less than the minimum wage, and more than 1 million declare no income at all (SALA 1989; Schneider 1996: 145).

One of the problematic consequences of unequal land distribution is what large farmers decide to plant. Small farmers grow subsistence crops like beans and manioc to feed their families before selling any surplus, but *fazendeiros* prefer cash crops for export like sugar, soybeans, and coffee. The unequal distribution of land, then, means that less land is used to grow food for local consumption than if it were distributed more equitably. Thus, more land is used to grow soybeans for export than for the two most important staples of the Brazilian diet combined: rice and beans (Coelho 1996: 199).

Regional Inequality

The inequality in Brazil is itself unequally distributed, concentrated in the northeast coast and *sertão* regions. The average monthly income in the northeast is $107, just 50 percent of the national average and only 40 percent of the average in the industrialized southeast. In fact, every other region has an average income at least twice as high as that found in the northeast (Coelho 1996: 33).

What is perhaps surprising about this regional inequality is that historically the northeast was the wealthiest, most productive region. Profits, however, were rarely invested either in modernizing sugar production or in industry. Thus, the northeast's economic problems represent in exaggerated form the obstacles Brazil faces in realizing its economic potential. To develop an economy that provides a decent standard of living for everyone, Brazil must find a way to distribute its resources more equitably and to ensure that the desire to export does not overwhelm the needs of local consumers.

Implementing an economic project of growth with equity will be difficult. Wealthy Brazilians benefit from the status quo and use their political power to oppose significant reforms, and the IMF opposes any reform that might disrupt the flow of Brazilian capital to foreign banks. Thus, economic problems are also political problems. Those who benefit and those who are harmed by the current economic system turn to the state to protect their economic interests. The struggles to implement alternative economic policies are sometimes violent because they are grounded in the inequality at the basis of the Brazilian economy.

CONCLUSION

The Brazilian economy is characterized by three basic continuities: (1) a high level of inequality between classes and between regions, (2) economic instability in which rapid growth (boom) is followed by collapse (bust), and (3) dependence on external markets for buyers, capital, and technology.

These continuities originated in the period of Portuguese colonization. The primary goal was to extract profit from Brazil by exporting goods to Europe. To maximize profits, the Portuguese relied on slave labor, initiating the economic inequality that plagues the Brazilian economy. They also focused on the production of a few cash crops, leaving the economy vulnerable to collapse when demand fell. The combination of inequality and lack of diversification has meant that Brazil has been unable to generate internally the markets, capital, and technology needed to sustain economic growth.

These three continuities are interconnected and therefore difficult to eliminate. The most significant attempt to transform the Brazilian economy occurred in 1929–64 when the government pursued import substitution industrialization (ISI). ISI successfully industrialized and diversified the economy, but it was limited by the small size of the internal market. Attempting to break out of this bottleneck, the government since 1964 has reopened the economy to the international market.

The Brazilian economy has certainly changed. Agricultural products like coffee and sugar no longer drive economic growth. Brazil is now the major industrial economy in South America, producing airplanes and computers. Yet with industrialization, inequality has worsened. The economy is still prone to boom and bust, as evidenced by the recession of the 1980s following the economic miracle of the late 1960s and early 1970s. Dependence on the international economy persists as well; oil price increases in the 1970s, the debt crisis of the 1980s, and the imposition of austerity packages by the IMF in the 1990s all demonstrate Brazil's vulnerability to external economic forces.

The Brazilian economy is full of contradictions: First World industry and Third World poverty, miraculous economic growth followed by stagnation. There are no easy solutions, but addressing the problem of inequality is fundamental. Both modernization and dependency perspectives agree that income redistribution would expand the internal market for Brazilian industrial goods, reducing the economy's external dependence. Although, redistribution might solve some economic problems, politically it is problematic and therefore highly unlikely, as will be seen in the following chapter.

CHAPTER 5

The Brazilian Political System

On March 31, 1964, the army high command sent tanks and troops into the streets to overthrow the democratic government of President João Goulart. In the preceding months, Goulart, a former labor minister supported by an increasingly militant union movement, had advocated serious land reform and restrictions on foreign capital. The military, deeply suspicious of Goulart and his agenda, claimed that a coup was necessary to protect Brazilian democracy from communist infiltration.

It was not a little ironic, then, that in the 1989 presidential election following more than two decades of military rule, one of the two candidates qualifying for the second round of voting was Lula, of the Workers' Party (PT). Introduced in the previous chapter, Lula had worked in São Paulo's auto industry since he was 14 years old. Radicalized by falling wages and union repression by the military government, he had become the leader of the militant metalworkers. In 1980, Lula gained national prominence when he was arrested by the military for leading a strike against the foreign-owned auto industry. Responding to the demand for a political party representing workers, Lula helped found the PT (Morel 1989).

The military had banned presidential elections for nearly 30 years precisely to prevent someone like Lula from coming to power. Thus, Brazilians anxiously awaited the outcome of the second round of voting. Lula lost the election but received a higher percentage of the vote (47 percent) than any leftist candidate in South American history. Decades of military rule had done little to eliminate the political challenge to Brazil's highly unequal distribution of wealth.

The winning candidate could not have presented a more glaring contrast to Lula. Fernando Collor de Mello was a political insider—university educated, member of a wealthy and politically powerful northeastern family, the governor of Alagoas. Lula was stocky and bearded, whereas Collor was tall and athletic with a wife as photogenic as himself. The ideal media candidate, Collor was heavily promoted by the largest television network in the country (Globo). Collor's campaign offered few concrete proposals for solving economic and social problems, but he was touted as a fierce enemy of the pervasive political corruption. Three years into his presidency, however, Collor was impeached for massive corruption in a scandal that began with public accusations by his own brother.

In 1994, Lula once again came in second in the presidential race when Brazilians opted for a sociologist, Fernando Henrique Cardoso. Cardoso had earned international recognition as one of the founders of dependency theory with his research on Latin American economies (Cardoso and Faletto 1979). He argued that Latin American economic development had been inhibited by the economies of Europe and North America. Cardoso had been forced into exile after the military coup of 1964.

Ironically, Cardoso was elected president primarily because as finance minister in 1993 he broke the inflation that had reached 2,670 percent by coupling the Brazilian currency to the U.S. dollar (Schneider 1996). As president, Cardoso appeared to further repudiate his earlier beliefs by privatizing state companies and opening up the Brazilian economy to increased foreign investment. His popularity, however, remained high during his first year in office as economic growth (5 percent in 1995) finally surpassed the rate of inflation (2.5 percent).

A SOCIOLOGICAL ANALYSIS OF BRAZILIAN POLITICS

How are we to understand these twists and turns of Brazilian politics? A military dictatorship "protects" democracy by overthrowing it. An arrested factory worker nearly becomes president. An enemy of corruption is impeached for corruption. A critic of foreign influence becomes president by tying Brazil's currency to the U.S. dollar. Is it possible that any thread connects these events, that a pattern underlies these seeming contradictions?

Some sociologists focus on the conflictual relations between those contending for power and conclude that the process is so complex that there is no underlying pattern and therefore political processes are basically unpredictable (O'Donnell and Schmitter 1986). When democracy does occur, it must be because powerful **elites** have compromised their differences (Higley and Burton 1989). In this view, the poor majority of Brazilians are largely irrelevant to the political process.

Other sociologists believe that despite the surface instability of politics, there is a stable, underlying pattern, just as in the economic sphere the surface turbulence of boom and bust veiled the persistence of inequality and external dependence. The parallel between the economic and political spheres is not by chance. The political conflicts grow out of an economy that does not consistently generate sufficient resources for all Brazilians. Thus, politics is patterned by **class** conflicts that are predictable (Neuhouser 1998).

Brazilian politics are hotly contested, with radically different visions of what role government should play. Should government protect those who own property or redistribute property to those without it? Should government promote industrialization; if so, what kind and who should pay for it? Can foreign capital assist economic **development** or does it exploit Brazilian resources?

Whether the primary conflicts are among elite groups or between classes, whether these conflicts are predictable or unpredictable, it's clear that the economic elites have dominated the political sphere, successfully defeating every challenge from below. They have used the Brazilian state to protect their interests, preserving their wealth at the cost of widespread poverty, economic and political instability, and dependence on foreign economies.

ORIGINS OF THE BRAZILIAN POLITICAL SYSTEM

From the beginning, Brazilian politics and economics have been so intertwined as to be virtually indistinguishable. The colony was divided into captaincies as large as medium-sized European countries and donated to a small number of individuals. The recipients of royal generosity were responsible both for the profitability of their landholdings and for maintaining social order. Given the great distance from Portugal, making communication slow and uncertain, the Portuguese crown resisted but could not prevent a great deal of local political autonomy.

Patron–Client Relations

During the colonial period, the large landowners confronted two major threats to social order. The first was the external threat of war with indigenous tribes and Dutch invaders. Unable to rely on the Portuguese to protect them, *fazendeiros* raised their own local armies. Using their monopoly on economic resources, they became **patrons** providing access to land or work to **clients** in exchange for their loyalty. In recognition of their semimilitary function, *fazendeiros* became known as colonels, though they often held no official position in the colonial army.

This **patron–client system** still structures relations in Brazil. The poor majority can only access what they need to survive by offering labor and loyalty to those who monopolize resources (Scheper-Hughes 1992). In rural areas, *fazendeiros* are commonly referred to with a mixture of admiration and fear as colonels. In the cities, the more urbane title of "doctor" is used to show respect to anyone with sufficient wealth and education to be a potential source of work or money. In both settings, the relationship is understood to be more than economic (exchanging work for wages); there is an implicit duty to defend the political interests of the patron. The Indian and Dutch threats are long gone, but loyal followers are still useful during elections and to defend the *fazendeiro*'s interests whenever and however necessary.

Despite the overt display of respect and submission by clients, power cannot buy love, and many clients deeply resent their dependence on and control by powerful patrons. Unable or unwilling to risk direct confrontation, clients often employ the **weapons of the weak,** publicly expressing deference and loyalty, but privately seeking ways to gain more than they give in the relationship (Scott 1985). Resistance to landlord domination raises the second problem of social control: how to contain the internal threat of rebellion against the hierarchical system.

Coerced Labor

Workers in Brazil rarely have been free. Colonial plantations were worked by slaves who escaped whenever they could; and when they couldn't escape (understandably), they worked only as hard as they could be forced to work. *Fazendeiros* used favored clients as overseers and guards to force slaves to exert themselves. The *fazendeiro* was the entire legal system—judge, jury, police, even executioner—who could determine guilt and render punishment with minimal constraint, not just for slaves but for all who fell within his economic realm. Portugal tried to limit the *fazendeiros'* power, but their isolation and private armies severely limited royal control.

Brazil continues to struggle with the twin problems of **coerced labor** and private justice. The number of reports of forced labor confirmed by the Pastoral Land Commission of the Roman Catholic Church soared from 4,883 in 1991 to 25,193 three years later. Brazilian sociologist José de Souza Martins estimates that as many as 85,000 employers violate the law against forced labor (Schemo 1995). Debt is now the primary means of initiating coerced labor. Workers fall into debt to their employers and then are forced to continue working to pay off the debt; but wages are so low that workers often never get free.

On August 10, 1995, the *New York Times* reported the case of Valdo and Eliana da Silva, employees of Carmig, a company that produces charcoal (by burning logs in large outdoor ovens) for Brazilian steel factories. The company says that Eliana and Valdo owe $4,700 for food bought on credit from a store that passes the bills on to Carmig. In the 28 months the couple has worked for Carmig, they have never been paid because the company claims that their wages don't cover their food costs. It's unlikely that they will ever be able to pay off this debt, because it would require that the couple work for five months, without eating. Workers who run away are tracked down, beaten, and stripped of their few possessions as partial payment of their debt. So, the Silvas and others are forced to continue working; and the longer they work, the deeper in debt they fall. Although many Brazilian slaves had the opportunity to earn their freedom, this is an increasingly remote possibility for Eliana and Valdo (Degler 1971; Schemo 1995).

In response to this problem, President Cardoso appointed a commission with a budget of $290 million to investigate reports of coerced labor. Even the federal government, though, has little power to protect workers. Large landowners and employers like Carmig often have close ties to the local officials responsible for investigating and enforcing labor laws. For example, the mayor of the town where Carmig is located is himself the owner of a charcoal operation, and local inspectors, on the rare occasions that they actually visit work sites, warn the companies they are coming. Even well-intentioned officials lack the resources needed to make a dent in the problem.

Origins of a Weak Bureaucratic State

The weakness of the central government is a legacy of the colonial period. The Portuguese crown fought against the power of the *fazendeiros* by creating ever more elaborate layers of **bureaucracy** and law. Thus, the crown decreed limits on landowner abuse of slaves (not because the crown was so concerned with their well-being but to control the landowners), abolished the captaincy system, and sent countless delegations of officials commissioned to investigate, report, and punish violations of royal law. Because the king was far away in Lisbon, however, it was the rare royal official who did not soon realize that the easiest and most profitable strategy was to side with the local economic elite.

Thus, an oversized bureaucratic and legal system grew despite (actually because of) its ineffectiveness and corruption. More and more layers of law and bureaucracy were added in a vain attempt to gain control over the *fazendeiros* and the officials they had corrupted. Brazil continues to struggle with the burden of state institutions that are simultaneously too big and too weak. Sociologist Peter Evans (1995) recounts the Brazilian joke in which a lion escapes from the zoo and, to survive, begins devouring government bureaucrats. No one notices their absence, however, until the lion eats the one person in the government office who actually provided a useful service, the functionary responsible for serving coffee! During the military regime, a department of debureaucratization was created to try to rein in the expanding state. The joke (or reality?) was that it was the only efficient department—so it was abolished.

VIOLENCE IN BRAZIL

Although bureaucratic inefficiency and corruption are the butt of jokes, the consequences are anything but funny. Most Brazilians have little faith that government will act fairly or provide security. Thus, police and citizens alike attempt to implement justice themselves, outside the legal system. In doing so, however, a vicious cycle is initiated in which one illegal act provokes and justifies the next.

An incident illustrating this spiral of violence occurred in Caranguejo. A young man from the community was arrested for the rape and murder of a coworker because he had been accused of the crime by his employer. Lacking evidence, the police tortured the young man to extract a confession. They first beat him on the soles of his feet until he could not walk. Then they poured gasoline over him; when they lit a match, he confessed. His neighbors, though, didn't believe that he had committed the crime because he was hardworking and religious. They were convinced that the storeowner was guilty and made the accusation to protect himself. For some reason (no one knew why), the young man was released pending trial. The danger from the police had passed for the moment, but now he was in danger from the girl's family, who had no reason to trust the legal system to punish the person who had confessed to this horrible crime.

This is the everyday violence of Brazil—violent crime, abusive police, and vigilante justice. Sometimes this violence erupts in mass killings such as the murder of eight street kids sleeping on the steps of Candelária cathedral (July 27, 1993) or the massacre of 21 residents of a Rio *favela* by off-duty policemen (August 30, 1993). These horrific acts sporadically make headlines in the international press, but the reality is that violence is an all-too-normal part of life in Brazil.

If the problem were simply corrupt and brutal police abusing the human rights of poor Brazilians, at least it would be clearly defined. The issue is complex, however. Urban Brazilians live under the constant threat of robbery and assault. Anyone who has not been robbed is still a "virgin." Urban homes have become walled fortresses, with bars over the windows and surrounded by high walls topped with broken glass. Brazilians joke that the criminals run free while their victims are imprisoned in their own homes. Some wealthy Brazilians avoid the dangers of the streets altogether by flying to work and back by helicopter.

Police Violence

In this atmosphere of fear and tension, police killings of *marginais*, or marginals—a derogatory term for the poor who are assumed to be criminals—are often secretly approved. From 1987 to 1992, the number of civilians killed by police in the state of São Paulo jumped from 305 to 1,470, more than 4 every day. Most of these deaths occurred in metropolitan São Paulo (1,350), where the police caused 32.7 percent of all recorded violent deaths. According to police statistics, in the first six months of 1992, the police killed 660 people, while wounding only 89. The suspiciously high ratio of dead to wounded suggests that many killings were informal executions; during the same period only 1 policeman was killed and 38 were wounded (Americas Watch 1993).

Police victims are disproportionately poor, black, young, and male. Two studies in São Paulo found that over half the victims were black, even though 75 percent of the residents of the city are white. In a study of 4,000 police killings in São Paulo, 17 percent of the victims were minors. In Brazil as a whole, murder is the fourth leading cause of death some major cities. Many of these children are killed by off-duty policemen who are paid by local businessowners to eliminate thieves (Dimenstein 1991; Americas Watch 1993; IBGE 1995).

Assassination is not the only crime within police ranks. From 1987 to 1992, 1,323 members of the military police were found guilty of crimes, including murder, theft, kidnapping, corruption, and drug trafficking. While I was in Brazil in September 1997, police officers were involved in two prominent child-kidnapping cases. When the crime is committed during the exercise of police duties or with police-issue weapons, the case is heard by a military court, which is frequently reluctant to punish accused officers (Tinoco and Leite 1993).

Low salaries are identified as one of the major factors provoking police corruption. In August 1993, a corporal in the military police in Rio de Janeiro earned about $US 238, 56 percent of a police officer's salary of equivalent rank in Buenos Aires and 11 percent of a New York police officer's salary. In fact, the August paycheck for street sweepers in Rio was larger than for a police corporal (Tinoco and Leite 1993). Given the incentive to supplement their income to provide for their families, it is perhaps surprising that the level of police corruption is not higher (Americas Watch 1993).

Vigilante Violence

Afraid of both criminals and police, ordinary citizens sometimes take justice into their own hands. The number of mob lynchings of suspected criminals is on the rise. On September 5, 1993, three men attacked a woman in her Recife house; a neighbor saw it and called for help to stop the attack. By the time they entered the house, the woman was dead; the crowd reacted by stoning and beating the three men. When the police arrived, they were unable to stop the attack by more than 200 people. By the time reinforcements reached the scene, two of the men were dead and the third died on the way to the hospital.

The level of support for popular justice is indicated by two quotes in the local paper the next day. As might be expected, the son of the murdered woman affirmed that "violence must be fought with violence." The father of one of the men killed by the crowd, however, went even further: "The attitude of the population was just. My son and the other two deserved it. I also wanted to have participated in the beating" (*Jornal do Comércio* 1993).

An Arbitrary Legal System

There are no simple solutions to the violence because it is the result of conditions that have festered for 500 years. From its beginning, Brazil has been marked by the interplay between inequality and violence. To acquire wealth, Portuguese colonizers used violence against the indigenous peoples of Brazil and then the peoples of Africa. To retain that wealth, the elite today use violence to keep poor Brazilians from organizing. The rich use government (democratic or authoritarian) to maintain the inequality of the status quo. Neither the police nor the Brazilian population view the government as a source of justice. A folk saying declares, "For my friends everything; for my enemies the law!"

Application of the law is often capricious, so Brazilians believe that one can always *dar um jeito*, "find a way" around even the most plain legal restrictions. At one point, the visa extension request for my wife and me was rejected. Before leaving Brazil, we visited the family that I had lived with during my year as an exchange student. They were shocked that we had given up so easily. If we really wanted to stay, there is always a *jeito*; simply stay—by the time the government noticed that we hadn't left, the additional year we had requested would have passed. This orientation toward the law is described as *obedecer mas não cumprir*, "to obey but not comply." The government hadn't ordered us out of the country, so staying wouldn't be disobedience, even though it wasn't exactly compliance.

That the problem of violence originates in the Brazilian state was noted in an editorial in the news magazine *Veja* following the police massacre of 21 people in a Rio de Janeiro *favela*. The author, Marcos Sá Corrêa (1993), observed that during blackouts in U.S. cities such as New York (1977) and Chicago (1990), the urban population went on a rampage, setting fires, breaking windows, and robbing stores. When a blackout occurred in Rio in March 1993, however, not a single window was broken. Thus, according to Corrêa, the problem in Brazil is not that the population is out of control; the problem "is the disorder of the state."

POLITICAL INSTABILITY

On March 19, 1964, 500,000 people marched through the streets of São Paulo, demanding the overthrow of President João Goulart. Within two weeks, Goulart and democracy had been replaced by a military dictatorship. Twenty years later, an estimated one million protesters jammed the streets of Rio de Janeiro, demanding democracy's return. The military leaders did not yield completely, but they were forced to accept the indirect election of a civilian president, the first in 30 years.

Why did Brazilians ask for the military to intervene and then demand that they leave? Why have neither democratic nor authoritarian regimes proved stable in Brazil? Instability is especially surprising, given the underlying continuity of elite power in Brazilian politics. If economic elites have always exercised power in Brazil, why haven't they found a stable form through which to rule, be it democratic or authoritarian?

The fundamental problem is that the Brazilian economy generates contradictory pressures that neither democratic nor authoritarian regime officials can resolve. When the pressures under one regime become unmanageable, a transition occurs that relieves some pressures but provokes new pressures that eventually are equally destabilizing. The surface politics—crises, regime transitions, scandals, corruption—obscure the underlying continuities in the Brazilian political system.

Democracy: 1945–1964

Brazilian democracy had its origins in 1945, when the populist dictator Getúlio Vargas was overthrown. Just 13 percent of the population voted in the first election, however, as illiterates were ineligible. Over the next 15 years, as literacy increased among urban workers, the number of voters doubled from 6.2 to 12.6 million. The rural poor, though, remained largely marginal to the democratic process, either because of their continued illiteracy or because their votes were controlled by the landowners.

As urban workers increasingly exercised the right to vote, they used it to elect candidates supporting consumption demands (higher wages and benefits, and subsidized food and transportation). Thus, the Brazilian Workers' Party (PTB), the chief party of urban workers (especially after the Communist Party was outlawed in 1948), steadily increased its congressional representation, climbing from just 8 percent in 1945 to 27 percent in 1962 (see Figure 5–1). During the same period, the two principal conservative parties declined from 90 percent to 53 percent. By 1962, the PTB had the second largest delegation in Congress (Neuhouser 1990).

Urban workers used their growing political muscle to raise living standards. The government doubled the real value of the minimum wage between 1945 and 1957 in the states of São Paulo and Rio de Janeiro. Raising wages was feasible, because it also benefited Brazilian industrialists. As explained in Chapter 4, Brazil was engaged in a process of import substitution industrialization, or ISI, in which higher wages stimulated demand for manufactured goods. Thus, industrialists tolerated higher wages as long as they spurred economic growth.

The completion of ISI in the early 1960s, however, ended the tacit political alliance between workers and industrialists, as growth stalled and inflation rose. If ISI were to generate further growth, rural workers had to be integrated into the consumer market. Paying rural workers more might stimulate further industrialization, but it was opposed by *fazendeiros* who would have to pay the costs (wages and land redistribution) but not reap the profits from selling manufactured consumer goods.

The stage was set for a political crisis. In 1961, João Goulart of the PTB became president. As a former minister of labor, Goulart had authorized significant wage increases. With strong labor union support, Goulart called for basic reforms, proposing the expropriation of land not

FIGURE 5-1

Change in Voter Participation and Congressional Results, 1945–1962

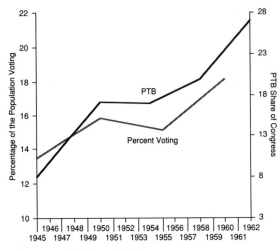

Source: McDonald and Ruhl (1989); Neuhouser (1990).

utilized by *fazendeiros* and distribution to the landless. To spur further industrialization, he restricted the ability of foreign firms to send profits made in Brazil outside the country. He also threatened nationalization of certain industries.

Because the PTB did not have a congressional majority to implement these basic reforms, Goulart sought to expand his constituency by promoting the unionization of rural workers and proposing a constitutional amendment to give illiterates the right to vote. In the first 15 years of democratic government only 6 rural unions had gained legal status, but in 1961–63 Goulart's administration recognized 260 new rural unions. If Goulart could organize rural workers and give them the vote, he would have the power to implement the basic reforms.

The economic elites, rural and industrial, felt increasingly threatened. The democratic process seemed to swing the balance of power to workers because their numbers gave them more votes. If voting was extended to rural workers, the elites feared that they would be politically marginalized, unable to use the state to protect their economic interests. From the point of view of the Brazilian elite, if democracy could not protect their interests, then democracy would have to go.

The *Estado do São Paulo* newspaper—the elite's "most representative mouthpiece" (Therborn 1979: 106)—labeled Goulart a communist and a threat to democracy. Goulart responded by escalating his own rhetoric; at a rally with 150,000 supporters in Rio de Janeiro on March 13, 1964, he signed a decree nationalizing oil refineries and another authorizing the expropriation of underutilized land. Goulart also called for the relegalization of the Communist Party (Neuhouser 1990).

Six days later an estimated half million people joined an anti-Goulart march in São Paulo, ending with a mass dedicated to the preservation of democracy by overthrowing it before the communists could take it over. A week later, thousands of sailors went on strike after their union leaders were arrested. When the insubordinant sailors were granted amnesty, the military was convinced that Goulart's mobilization of workers was too dangerous to continue. On March 31, army troops and tanks patrolled the streets and Goulart fled into exile (Skidmore 1967; Stepan 1971; Flynn 1978; Neuhouser 1990).

Military Dictatorship: 1964–1985

The military regime's first order of business was to eliminate the democratic political spaces in which workers had pushed their consumption demands. During "operation cleanup," the military arrested an estimated 50,000 "subversives," union leaders and leftist politicians. Others were picked up by the military, tortured, and sometimes "disappeared" (killing a person in custody, hiding the corpse, and then denying all knowledge). The PTB was outlawed, its congressional delegation removed from office and denied the right to run for reelection or vote. Union leaders in 70 percent of the large unions (more than 5,000 members) were removed; 90 percent of the rural unions organized in 1963–64 were terminated (Alves 1985).

The military regime then turned its attention to the economic crisis caused by stalled growth and inflation that threatened to surpass 100 percent. The option of resolving the crisis by extending ISI by integrating rural workers into the consumer market had been rejected along with the democratic regime. The military opted instead for a dual-pronged strategy of deepening industrialization by developing a capital goods sector (goods used in the production of consumer goods) and promoting the export of manufactured goods.

To pay for deepening and to make manufactured exports competitive, the military regime suppressed workers' wages. Dr. Mário Simonsen, minister of finance during the 1970s, claimed that the regime's wage policy

> served to simplify and pacify wage-claim negotiations; these are no longer resolved by rounds of strikes, and other forms of collective pressure, but simply by rapid mathematical calculations (Flynn 1978: 392).

In fact, the government consistently underestimated inflation and productivity so that the "rapid mathematical calculations" cheated the workers out of cost-of-living and productivity increases. As a result, the real value of the minimum wage fell 36 percent from 1965 to 1976 (Alves 1985). Reduced labor costs benefited industrialists with more capital for investment and more competitive prices for Brazilian exports.

Falling wages helped fuel rapid growth during the economic miracle of the late 1960s and early 1970s, but it came at a cost. The first cost was worsening income inequality. Thus, the local market for manufactured goods remained small relative to Brazil's population size. The second cost was that dependence on external markets for capital, technology, and exports increased Brazil's vulnerability to changes in external markets, such as rising interest rates on foreign debt and reduction in demand for exports. The military regime's economic policies spurred short-term growth but intensified fundamental structural weaknesses of the economy.

As long as the world economy grew, the economy's weaknesses remained hidden and political opposition to the military regime minimized. In the mid-1970s, however, OPEC shocked the world by raising oil prices. Brazil produced only 21 percent of the oil it consumed, so rising oil prices doubled its import bill and reignited inflation. U.S. inflation drove up interest rates on Brazil's foreign debt, making repayment increasingly difficult (Baer 1983; Coelho 1996). As the world slipped into recession in the early 1980s, demand for Brazil's exports fell. Unable to pay its debts or purchase imports, the economy collapsed and with it went the last vestiges of popular support for the military regime.

Opposition came initially from workers whose wages were falling. Workers risked the wrath of the military by engaging in illegal strikes. In 1978, 24 strikes involved 500,000 workers; the next year the number of strikes jumped to 113, with three million participants. By 1983 the number of labor disputes (strikes and lockouts) reached 312 (Alves 1985; SALA 1989). Workers under the leadership of Lula and other labor activists also organized the Workers' Party; for the first time, Brazilian workers controlled their own political representation (Morel 1989).

Worker resistance to the military regime was predictable; more surprising was the growing opposition of the economic elite. The first capitalists to express discontent were manufacturers producing for the local market because demand for their products was limited by the regime's wage-constraint policy. With the economic problems of the 1970s and early 1980s, capitalists in general lost confidence that the government's economists knew what they were doing. Because the regime was a dictatorship and didn't have to listen to civilian complaints no matter how wealthy the critics, even the elites began demanding democratization (Smith and Turner 1984; Neuhouser 1990).

Congressional elections reflected declining support for the dictatorship. The president and mayors of major cities were appointed, but elections to a weakened Congress continued. The regime permitted only two parties to function: the proregime ARENA (National Renovating Alliance) and the opposition MDB (Brazilian Democratic Movement). From 1970 to 1978, ARENA congressional representation fell from 72 percent to 55 percent (see Figure 5–2). In 1982, the progovernment party won only 49 percent of the congressional seats, but it maintained a Senate majority because the electoral rules were so biased that the party won 67 percent of the Sen-

FIGURE 5–2

Congressional Election Results during Military Regime,
1970–1982

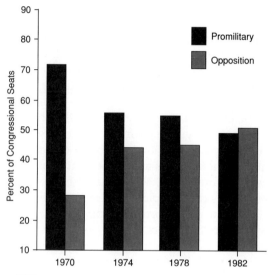

Source: Neuhouser (1990).

ate races with only 39 percent of the total vote (*Encyclopaedia Britannica Book of the Year* 1986; IBGE 1995).

By the early 1980s, the military regime had virtually no civilian support and appeared unable to solve the economic crisis. As protests multiplied, regime officials sought to script the most dignified retreat possible. The military rejected demands for a direct presidential election, but in 1985 it did allow Congress to indirectly choose a civilian president from the opposition. After 21 years of military rule, democracy had a second chance to tackle the country's problems.

CONTEMPORARY DEMOCRACY: 1985 TO THE PRESENT

Democracy is back, but the dilemma remains: how to reconcile a political system intending to disperse power equally to all with an economic system concentrating wealth in the hands of the few. Won't poor Brazilians again use their voting rights to elect candidates promising to redistribute economic benefits to the poor? Won't the economic elite again try to use government to protect their privileged economic position? If the poor succeed in turning ballots into political power, will this be tolerated by the wealthy or will they once again overthrow democracy? If the elite manipulate the democratic process to prevent the poor majority from ruling, is the system really democratic?

In the presidential election of 1989 (the first since 1960), these questions were given provisional answers. The two candidates in the final round of voting (no candidate received a majority in the first round, so the top two advanced to a second round) offered voters two distinct options. Lula, the union activist and candidate of the Workers' Party, advocated a platform that envisioned greater economic equality: "I defend private property, but for everybody. We cannot allow one man to own 25 million acres when others are starving" (Powers 1994: 16). Collor, member of a wealthy, elite family, avoided questions of redistribution, preferring to focus on the problem of political corruption, trusting the free market to solve problems of inequality.

The economic elites supported Collor and they had a powerful new tool to bolster his candidacy: television. In 1970, there were only 6.1 million TVs in Brazil; 15 years later there were an estimated 25 million. By 1993, 76 percent of all households and 85 percent of all urban households owned a TV. Even in rural areas, 40 percent of households own a television, and this number is rising rapidly (SALA 1989: 78; IBGE 1995: 2–213). Satellite technology now makes broadcasting possible into even the most remote areas, where satellite dishes are increasingly common. By the mid-1980s, there were more than three times as many TVs as newspapers per capita (SALA 1989: 72, 78). The difference in influence is even greater, as more people watch each TV than read each newspaper. The dominant player is Roberto Marinho, owner of the Globo network, which included 54 local stations in 1987 (of a total 123 commercial stations in 1983) and regularly had weeknight audiences of 60 to 80 million viewers (SALA 1989: 77; Kottak 1992: 277; Page 1995: 173).

Marinho threw the power of his media empire into Collor's campaign. When the campaign began, Collor was virtually unknown, the governor of a small, poor state, far from the power centers of Rio, São Paulo, and Brasília. The Collor family, however, owned a television station in the Globo network, and Marinho had been a business partner of Collor's father. Collor took advantage of the opportunities Marinho provided to project his charisma through the television screen, coming from nowhere to easily win the first round of voting (Page 1995). During the second round, the government strictly controlled TV access, but Marinho manipulated Globo's news coverage to portray Collor favorably and to depict Lula negatively (Powers 1994: 20; Page 1995: 173).

Globo's support proved just enough, as Collor captured 53 percent of the valid votes. In defeat, Lula received the largest popular vote (47 percent) of any leftist presidential candidate in Latin American history. The elites heaved a collective sigh of relief, but their satisfaction with Collor was short-lived. Having delivered the presidency to him, the elite expected Collor to defend their economic interests; instead, Collor used his office to advance his personal interests. After his own brother publicly accused him of corruption, a congressional investigation estimated that Collor illegally pocketed $55 million in his first two years in office (Torregrosa 1993: 134). On September 29, 1992, the Chamber of Deputies suspended Collor from office and began the impeachment process. Three months later, after less than three years in office, Collor resigned. Brazil's first democratically elected president since 1960 became the first, and only, president in the western hemisphere to be impeached (Burns 1993: 484).

Vice president Itamar Franco served as interim president until the scheduled elections of 1994. Lula was the early front-runner, leading preference polls. Hyperinflation—2,670 percent in 1993—threatened to consume working-class salaries and seemed to confirm Lula's criticism of the government and its economic policies. Nine months before the election, the cover of the *Los Angeles Times Magazine* (March 27) showed a close-up of Lula with the teaser, "The leftist presidential candidate has the scandal-ridden establishment running scared."

This changed in mid-1994, however, when the minister of finance and soon-to-be presidential candidate Fernando Henrique Cardoso introduced a new currency linked to the U.S. dollar. This, in combination with the elimination of deficit financing by the government, helped lower inflation from 760 percent in the first half of the year to only 22 percent in the second half (Schneider 1996: 153). Cardoso rode a wave of popularity to surge from behind to capture the presidency in the first round with 54 percent, while Lula rapidly faded to 27 percent (SALA 1996).

Cardoso, a former leftist sociologist exiled after the 1964 military coup, now seems convinced that a strong economy will trickle down to Brazil's poor. Apparently contradicting his earlier views, Cardoso sold off state industries and promoted integration into the international market. Although heavily criticized by the left, which underestimated the importance of low inflation to the workers, Cardoso's early popularity was so high that there was talk of changing the constitution to allow him to run for reelection. At the end of 1997, however, stock market collapses in Asia reverberated around the globe, threatening Brazil's economy. Once again, Brazil's economic exposure to international market forces that it does not control is all too evident. In response, Cardoso was forced into another round of fiscal belt-tightening, cutting social services and laying off government employees, a strategy that once again forces Brazil's poor to pay the costs of the country's economic vulnerability.

THE MEANING OF BRAZILIAN DEMOCRACY

Most poor Brazilians hold very pragmatic views of democracy. Rather than seeing the electoral process as a way to address national issues, they use democracy to solve more immediate and personal problems. Given that significant change in the status quo has always been blocked and their day-to-day situation is often desperate, this attitude is quite rational.

In Caranguejo, I saw this pragmatic orientation up close. My neighbors were convinced that the only power they held in the electoral process was their vote and that the power of the vote disappeared after it was cast because the voter had no more influence over the candidate. Thus, Caranguejo residents sought to maximize the power of their vote *prior* to the election. Candidates made donations to soccer clubs in return for votes, and one provided materials for a bridge across the canal dividing the community. One woman received a tubal ligation for recruiting 10 voters for a candidate. This behavior might shock Americans, but my neighbors would be equally shocked by our hopelessly naive belief that politicians should be responsive to voters *after* they are elected.

Although the poor receive some concrete benefits from the electoral process (more frequent elections mean more frequent benefits), this behavior reinforces the status quo. Because of the expense of delivering benefits to voters prior to taking office, only incumbents (with access to government funds) and the wealthy (using personal resources) are able to run successful campaigns. Candidates like Lula who attempt to focus attention on national problems are criticized by poor voters for being stingy, failing to offer even T-shirts and barbecues to reward supporters.

The PT, however, tries to transmit a different vision of the possibilities of democratic politics. In one meeting, I watched a PT congressional candidate patiently explain to residents in Caranguejo that although he couldn't solve their local drainage problems, in Congress he could address national problems like wage policy and workers' rights. The PT appears to be making slow headway. In the first elections that it contested (1982), the PT won 6 seats in the national Congress; in 1994, the party claimed 55 seats, 10.6 percent of the total. The PT helped elect the first black woman to Congress (1986), Benedita da Silva, a resident of a Rio *favela*. Three years later, the PT's Luiza Erundina became the first Marxist mayor of São Paulo (Page 1995; SALA 1996). The question remains, however: If poor Brazilians do exercise their democratic rights, will the economic elite tolerate majority rule or will they once again betray Brazilian democracy?

CONCLUSION

The contemporary Brazilian political system is rooted in the colonial era in which government was weak as a result of the distance from Portugal and the power of *fazendeiros*. In response, the crown added layers of bureaucracy in a vain attempt to exert control. As a result, the Brazilian state, paradoxically, is both too large and too weak. An ineffective but demanding state provoked a vicious cycle of escalating state, criminal, and vigilante violence. A legal system that acts illegally appears arbitrary and illegitimate. In fact, to the extent that the state functions, it is primarily to defend the interests of wealthy and powerful Brazilians, so solving fundamental problems like poverty and inequality becomes nearly impossible. As a result, Brazil has experienced political instability, with swings from democracy to dictatorship and back. Brazil is once again democratic, but it is unclear if the current government will be any more successful in reconciling the egalitarian thrust of democracy with the inertia of economic inequality.

CHAPTER 6

Urbanization in Brazil

Under the cover of darkness on a Friday night in late March 1971, a woman hastily erected a shack along the bank of a newly constructed canal in Recife. Niçinha and her family had been threatened with eviction from their rented room because they owed several months' back rent. Desperately afraid of being forced out on the street with her children, Niçinha finally convinced her husband to confront the perils of invasion.

Niçinha built on land belonging to the Navy, and the military regime was strongly opposed to urban land invasions. In many other instances, the military police had driven invaders from their shacks with batons, German shepherds, and tear gas. Niçinha, however, had timed her invasion well. With government offices closed for the weekend, she had until Monday morning to establish herself on the land. The weekend also gave other people in similar circumstances time to follow her example. By Monday morning there were several dozen shacks along the canal.

On Monday, the military police arrived and tore down the shacks, throwing the wood into the canal. Some invaders fled, but Niçinha and other women stayed. To protect their homes, they gathered their children and challenged the police: "If you're going to tear down our houses, then you'll have to tear it down on top of us!" Apparently unwilling to risk killing women and children, the officers left these houses standing. After the police left, those who had run away returned, pulled the wood out of the canal, and rebuilt their shacks. This conflict repeated itself several times over the following days, until the police and city officials gave up in frustration.

This community, named Caranguejo after the little crabs that abound in the area, has changed dramatically since 1971. The invasion steadily expanded into the surrounding marshlands; by 1997, it contained approximately 4,000 people. Despite opposition from the city government, Caranguejo's residents have struggled to improve their community. The first invaders built precarious shacks of wood scraps, plastic, and cardboard on stilts to elude the tides that flooded the area; today over 90 percent of the houses are brick and innumerable truck-loads of dirt have raised the entire area above even the highest tides. At first, residents had to carry water from a public water fountain in an ad-jacent neighborhood, but now almost all houses are connected to the city's water and electric lines.

Despite many improvements, the community's most basic problem seemed beyond the residents' ability to solve: sewage disposal. Caranguejo was originally below sea level, and there was no easy way to remove waste sanitarily, so it was dumped in the canal that cut through the community. The saving grace was that daily tides flushed out the canal. Even so, conta-minated water was a serious health hazard. I was astounded, then, when I visited Caranguejo in 1997 and found the state building a sewer system to serve about half the community. Residents claimed that they were no longer living in a *favela*.

Caranguejo's history is typical of the **urbanization** that is trans-forming Brazil. The major coastal cities have been overwhelmed by ex-tremely rapid growth, fueled by massive migration from rural areas. Poor migrants, seeking a better life in the cities, arrived lacking the basic resources necessary for survival. Neither the government nor the market provided the jobs, houses, schools, and so forth that were necessary to meet the migrants' needs. In this context, migrants struggled to build what they needed from scratch, often outside the formal, legal channels established by the government. They invaded land for housing; they tapped city water and power lines without permission; they established their own schools and health clinics.

Despite the many critical problems that remain (high unemployment, infant mortality, and hunger), the residents of Caranguejo miraculously have carved out lives for themselves in an inhospitable urban environ-ment. Their achievements suggest that Brazil's urban problems can be solved. Yet, during the years that this one community struggled to im-prove, hundreds of new invasions occurred, multiplying the magnitude of the problem. Recife now has over 500 *favelas,* where more than 60 percent of the people crowd onto 10 percent of the urban space (ETAPAS 1991).

As a result, Recife is Brazil's poorest city; nearly half its residents fall below the government-defined line of absolute poverty. In 1991, Recife was ranked fourth worst in quality of life in the world; only the capitals of Bangladesh (Dhaka), Nigeria (Lagos), and Zaire (Kinshasa) received worse rankings (ETAPAS 1991). The problems of uncontrolled urbaniza-tion may be most glaring in Recife, but they are present in all Brazilian cities. Figure 6–1 reports the poverty rates in major Brazilian cities in 1989.

RAPID URBANIZATION

Historically, colonial cities were small, limited primarily to two func-tions: trade and administration. The majority of the population was

FIGURE 6—1

Poverty Rates in Major Brazilian Cities, 1989

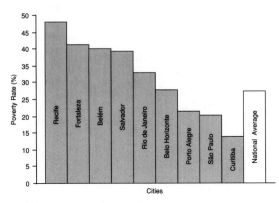

Source: ETAPAS (1991).

rural producing most of what they needed to survive and importing anything else. In 1872, only 10 cities had even 30,000 residents and just 3—Rio, Recife, and Salvador—had populations exceeding 100,000 (Coelho 1996: 324).

Little had changed by the turn of the century. Only one more city—São Paulo—claimed 100,000 inhabitants. After 1940, however, as industrialization accelerated, the cities exploded, growing almost three times as rapidly as the rural population (Smith 1963: 597). Even so, in 1960 a majority of Brazilians still lived in rural areas. The 1991 census, however, reported that three of every four Brazilians lived in cities. Today, 15 metropolitan regions have more than a million residents (Schneider 1996: 2–3). Amazingly, even in the Amazon, a majority of the population (59 percent) is urban (IBGE 1995).

Brasília

No city better exemplifies the speed of urbanization than the national capital. In 1955, Brasília literally didn't exist; it was a cow pasture in the state of Goias and a dream in the heads of a few politicians and urban planners. Since colonization, Brazil's population had been concentrated within a few miles of the Atlantic coast, while the vast interior was largely ignored. To stimulate the development of the interior, President Kubitschek determined to shift the national capital 575 miles inland from Rio de Janeiro.

Just three years after construction began, Brasília was inaugurated as the new national capital in April 1960. Designed to exemplify the ideal future Brazilians dreamed for their country, the capital instead reveals the deep-rooted divisions in Brazilian society. City plans included ultramodern housing and offices for government workers but no housing for the laborers without whom Brasília would not have been built. Surrounding the city, then, are *favelas* known as "anti-Brasílias."

Brasília represents two great ironies. First, the planned Brasília is criticized for being un-Brazilian because of its inhuman, massive scale and repetitive architecture, while the anti-Brasílias display the spontaneity and creativity of the Brazilian people. Second, the government bureaucrats for whom the city was built had to be enticed away from Rio de Janeiro by doubling their salaries, while the construction workers excluded from the plans were drawn only by the elusive hope of employment.

Regardless of the failures of the urban planners, Brasília's growth has been incredibly rapid. In the year it was inaugurated, Brasília already was home to 140,000 residents. Twenty years later, the population surpassed one million. By 1991, 31-year-old metropolitan Brasília was the ninth largest city in Brazil, with 1.8 million residents (IBGE 1995; Schneider 1996: 3).

MIGRATION

Brazil's rapid urbanization has been fueled by migration. From 1940 to 1991, the population increased by 105.9 million; 92 percent of this growth was urban; only 8 percent was rural. Because both urban **mortality** and **fertility rates** are lower than in the countryside, the disparity in growth rates was caused primarily by millions of rural Brazilians—like Lula and his family—abandoning the country for the city. In just 40 years (1940–80), an astounding 48 million Brazilians left their homes in search of a better life somewhere else (Coelho 1996).

Since 1940, most migrants have come from the *sertão* and the northeast coast. From 1940 to 1980, these two regions had a net out-migration of 12.9 million people. No other region had a net loss as a result of migration (Coelho 1996: 312). Initially, the favored destinations were the southern industrial cities. At its peak during the 1970s, as many as 600,000 migrants arrived *each year* in the São Paulo metropolitan region alone (Roberts 1978: 89).

As the coastal cities filled up, migrants turned their attention toward the cities of the rapidly developing agricultural heartland. Goiânia, the capital of Goias, had a population of 53,000 in 1950, but nearly one million (922,000) 41 years later, a phenomenal growth rate of 1,640 percent. The capitals of Mato Grosso (Cuiabá) and Mato Grosso do Sul (Campo Grande) both nearly doubled in size in the 11 years between the census counts of 1980 and 1991 (IBGE 1995).

Impetus for Migration

Historically, Brazil experienced intermittent bursts of migration caused by economic **boom and bust** and the periodic droughts that castigate the *sertão*. Since 1940, however, the rural population has been steadily

TABLE 6–1

Population Growth in Principal Capital Cities

City	1872	1940	1991
Belém	61,997	206,331	1,244,689
Belo Horizonte	*	211,377	2,020,161
Brasília	*	*	1,601,094
Campo Grande	*	*	526,126
Cuiabá	35,987	33,678	402,813
Curitiba	12,651	140,656	1,315,035
Forteleza	42.458	180,185	1,768,637
Goiânia	*	*	922,222
Manaus	29,334	106,399	1,011,501
Porto Alegre	43,998	272,232	1,263,403
Recife	116,671	348,424	1,298,229
Rio de Janeiro	274,972	1,764,141	5,480,768
Salvador	129,109	290,443	2,075,273
São Paulo	31,385	1,326,261	9,646,185
Average	77,856	443,648	2,184,010

*Either did not exist or was not a capital city in that year.
Source: IBGE (1995).

pushed out of the countryside. The primary cause has been the introduction of machinery by *fazendeiros* to increase agricultural efficiency. The number of tractors surged from just 61,000 in 1960 to 652,000 in 1985 (Coelho 1996: 198). **Mechanization** increased agricultural production; for example, grain production more than doubled from 1980–81 to 1994–95 (Schneider 1996: 145). One problem, though, is that it also drastically reduced the need for workers; the agricultural labor force fell from 52 percent of all workers in 1960 to only 23 percent in 1993 (SALA 1989, 1996). Unable to find farm work, millions of Brazilians had little choice but to head for the city. Table 6–1 shows the population growth of principal capital cities in Brazil.

Even for the employed rural population, life is hard. Rural wages average only one-third urban wages, and the indigence rate (defined as extreme/critical poverty) is 25 percent higher than in the cities. Malnutrition may be twice as high among the farmers that grow Brazil's food than it is for people living in the cities. In 1993, only 38 percent of rural houses had running water, compared to 88 percent of urban houses; 57 percent of rural households had electricity, compared to 98 percent of urban households. With most hospitals and schools located in the cities, the rural population has higher mortality and illiteracy rates than the urban residents. It is not surprising, then, that the greatest net out-migration has been from the poverty-stricken northeast (IBGE 1995; SALA 1996).

To the impoverished rural population the city appears to be a promised land where life will be easier and more enjoyable. Rural migrants are astute, choosing cities that offer the greatest opportunities. Thus, during the rapid industrialization of the 1970s, São Paulo attracted the largest number of migrants. When industrial employment failed to keep pace with migration, migrants increasingly opted for the cities of the agricultural heartland.

In addition to the potential material advantages (jobs, schools, electricity), there is another attraction of the city that is in short supply in the countryside. Many migrants identify *movimento* (action) as a significant reason why they would never return to the country. Brazilians love being where the action is, and nowhere is there more than in the city. Thus, in contrast to what occurs in American cities, the working class tends to be relegated to the less-desirable outlying suburbs while the more active inner city is full of expensive high-rise apartment buildings for the wealthy.

THE INFORMAL ECONOMY

Despite carefully choosing destinations, the number of migrants completely overwhelmed the coastal cities. Brazil has an estimated urban housing deficit of 7.3 million dwellings, and officially unemployment was 15 percent in 1993; 25 million more workers have insufficient employment (ETAPAS 1991: 12; Soares 1995: 13; Schneider 1996: 173). Thus, for most migrants, there was neither housing nor employment to welcome their arrival.

Migrants had to solve the basic problems of survival on their own; and many did so by participating in the **informal economy** that exists outside the legally regulated markets. Informal jobs are illegal because of the nature of the work (robbery, prostitution, drug-dealing) or because it is performed in a technically illegal way (without a permit or payment of taxes, subminimum wages, underage workers). Free housing is acquired through invasion; schools and health clinics are run by communities without governmental support.

It is impossible to measure accurately the informal economy because it operates in the shadows, hidden from the view of official statistic takers. It is clear, though, that it is huge. In Recife, an estimated 51.5 percent of all workers in 1980 labored in the informal economy. Many of these informal workers are self-employed small-business owners and artisans. The sidewalks in the city center are covered by street vendors hawking everything imaginable, from homemade food to cell phones. At stoplights, children sell fruit to motorists or wash their windshields. These workers are vulnerable because the police periodically conduct sweeps, arresting and confiscating the merchandise of anyone who fails to run away quickly enough. In the early 1990s, a prosecutor in Recife tried to enforce the law against child labor by arresting children for working.

Many workers employed in apparently legitimate activities actually are in the informal sector because employers don't sign work cards to avoid contributing to employee pension and health care funds. In the depths of the 1980s recession, over 70 percent of the workforce may have been working without a signed work card (Schneider 1996: 171). One of my neighbors in Caranguejo—Carminha—worked informally as a maid and cook for 12 years because her employer refused to sign her work card. Finally, after much pressure, she agreed to sign but without acknowledging Carminha's years of service. In effect, Carminha was cheated out of a substantial portion of her retirement benefits.

FAVELAS

Poorly paid and frequently unemployed, the urban poor cannot afford legal housing and are faced with the choice between living on the street or invading unoccupied land. Official statistics don't exist on the homeless, but a late-night tour of any Brazilian city reveals countless people sleeping under bridges and on sidewalks beneath store awnings. Ten million children live on the street, and the number of adults is probably higher (Jeffrey 1995: 160).

Life on the streets is harsh, exposed to the violence of criminals and police, so the preference is to invade unoccupied land and erect a shack offering minimal protection. The 1991 census counted 3,183 *favelas* containing 3.1 percent of the population (IBGE 1995). The actual numbers are certainly much higher. Multiplying the estimated urban housing shortage (7.3 million) by the average number of residents per *favela* household (4.36) yields an estimate of 31.8 million people living in inadequate housing, 22 percent of the population. For metropolitan Recife, the census counted 156,000 residents living in 100 *favelas*. A more thorough survey, however, found 500 *favelas*, home to two million people, nearly half the census total for the entire country (ETAPAS 1991: 38).

An invasion provides rudimentary housing but little else. Essential infrastructure and social services are absent, and city governments don't want to reward invaders by providing them. Thus, services that most people take for granted—water, electricity, sewers, schools, garbage collection—are problems to be solved by the community itself. To get water, mains are dug up, holes drilled in existing pipes, and new pipes run to houses; to get electricity, wires are strung from nearby power lines. Until the utility companies notice, residents have free services. If the companies cut off the utilities, residents reconnect the lines after the inspectors leave. Usually the companies allow the pirate lines to stay, but charge a flat rate for use.

Social services are more difficult, often requiring years of struggle to acquire. Many *favelas* have organized neighborhood associations to represent community interests to the government and to mobilize residents to address community problems (Gay 1994). No health care was available in Caranguejo until, in the mid-1980s, UNESCO trained some local women as health agents to treat wounds, give vaccinations, and monitor infant

In the rapidly growing cities, space is at a premium. Here, invaders have built shacks so close together along the bank of a canal that the only place for children to play is in the canal itself.

growth. After the training, though, there was no governmental structure in which the women could work. For several years, the health agents provided free health care, working from a rented house they paid for themselves. To build a health clinic, the community raised money by holding yard sales, collecting recyclables, and asking families to donate 10 bricks. Between their own efforts and money raised by a Belgian journalist who visited the community, a clinic was built with a large waiting room, several examination rooms, and a pharmacy. After years of such sacrifice, the state finally sent doctors for the clinic and provided salaries for the health agents. The women now are state employees, yet they are working illegally because the state refused to sign their work cards. Regardless, the health agents significantly improved the community's health. There is nearly 100 percent provision of all childhood vaccines; infant mortality has dropped; medicines and birth control (pills, condoms) are distributed for free.

THE MYTH OF MARGINALITY

Clearly, the urban poor are structurally disadvantaged; they must struggle to access the resources and services that others receive as a matter of course. In addition, they are socially disadvantaged, stigmatized and discriminated against simply for being poor. In Recife there is a popular morning radio news program that dramatically reports all the worst crimes committed during the night. The poor, as perpetrators or victims, are commonly referred to as *marginais,* "marginals." This term is used to stigmatize the poor as only marginally human. Lacking the cultural refinements of the wealthy, they are perceived as existing on the margins of society, stereotyped as subhuman and threatening to "civilized" Brazilian society.

The perception of the urban poor as *marginais,* however, is a deceptive myth (Perlman 1976), distorting reality on at least three levels: (1) The urban poor are not marginally human; they exemplify some of the highest ideals of human culture. (2) The urban poor are not marginal economically; they contribute vital goods and services to the Brazilian economy. (3) The urban poor are not marginal culturally; they are the source of many of Brazil's most fundamental and prized cultural practices.

Contribution to Humanity

Despite the **myth of marginality,** the Brazilian poor embody some of the highest human ideals. In conditions so harsh that they would seem to compel selfish commitment to personal survival, I have never seen greater generosity of heart. Angela was a single mother with four children, who washed clothes by hand for sailors while their ships docked in the port. At times work was scarce and the only food she could offer her children was plain macaroni. Yet, when sailors sometimes gave her foreign canned food, Angela would bring it to my wife and I, sure that it was food that we missed from the United States.

At one entrance to the *favela* is a nice house rented out to a firm of engineers. One weekend, Maria, a homeless single mother, put up a shack in an open area owned by the city but where the engineers parked their cars. On Monday morning, the engineers arrived and, finding their parking space taken, complained to their landlord. The owner soon arrived with an off-duty policeman and began to scream at Maria, demanding that she tear down the shack. Dressed in nice clothes, with rings on her fingers, the owner was obviously a wealthy woman; yet she claimed that if the shack stayed she would be unable to rent the office space and therefore unable to feed her children.

A crowd soon gathered, and I fully expected them to respond with the outrage that I felt at this self-centered woman who wanted to put a family back on the street. My neighbors, though, were more forgiving. Instead of reacting in anger, they listened quietly. They attempted to reason with her, explaining how badly Maria and her children needed a place to live. Finally, as the woman was losing control, one person asked if she would like a chair so that she could sit down in the shade and regain her composure. They never acted disrespectfully, but they also didn't give in, and Maria still lives in her house at the entrance to the *favela.* If the owner hadn't been blinded by her stereotypes of *marginais,* she might have learned something that day about civilized behavior.

Economic Contribution

Also a myth is the belief that the urban poor do not contribute to the economy. If the poor ever were to disappear, wealthy Brazilians would find out how dependent their affluent lifestyles are on the existence of a large poor population serving them at very low cost. From birth, the wealthy are enveloped in the care provided by poor nannies, maids, and cooks. Rarely are they required to lift a finger to perform any strenuous or dirty manual labor. This service is so taken for granted that it is rarely acknowledged or even noticed. The availability of a poorly paid servant class affords a higher standard of living than would be possible in the United States at the same income level. For example, my host family during my student exchange year had less income than my American family, yet in the United States I had to wash dishes, do yard work, and make my bed; in Brazil the family's maid did all these things for me.

The urban poor also sustain the Brazilian economy. The informal economy provides many critical products and services efficiently and at very low cost. One common job for men in Caranguejo is to pull a heavy cart through the city streets and collect recyclable items (paper, cardboard, glass, metal) by sifting through trash. This work is exhausting, dangerous (maneuvering carts through city traffic), dirty, and apparently of little importance—after all, it's just trash. These independent recyclers, however, perform a valuable, though not valued, service. A whole recycling industry is dependent on these men, from the middlemen who buy the trash, to the businesses that recycle it, to the factories that find it cost-effective to purchase recycled materials. Thus, long before Americans began recycling for environmental reasons, poor Brazilians did it for economic reasons.

Cultural Contribution

The urban poor are not marginal culturally; they have created much of what is valued as being Brazilian. Soccer is the national passion, and perhaps nothing is more central to Brazil's self-image. Brazilians claim to have the best soccer in the world—Brazil is the only country to have won the World Cup four times, their 1998 national team was ranked number one in the world, and Ronaldo was just elected the world's best soccer player for the second year running. They also can lay legitimate claim to playing the world's most beautiful soccer. Brazil's teams and players are widely considered the most enjoyable to watch because their foot skills and creativity make it appear that they are dancing with the ball. One spectator at the 1994 World Cup observed that for the Europeans soccer is a war they must win, but for the Brazilians soccer is a *festa*, a celebration.

Brazil has the urban poor to thank for creating this distinctive and successful soccer. Pelé, voted the world's all-time greatest player, was shining shoes on the streets when he was seven. Romário, who led Brazil to the 1994 World Cup championship in Pasadena, grew up in a Rio *favela*. Brazilian soccer, with its emphasis on creativity and finesse, rather than brute force, to overcome the opponent, embodies the tactics of the urban poor (the indirect **weapons of the weak**) in their daily struggles to survive.

Soccer is indisputably the national pastime, but Carnival also can claim to being the national passion. During the days preceding Ash Wednesday and the beginning of Lent (pre-Easter period when devout Catholics deny themselves earthly pleasures), Brazilians celebrate on a scale unmatched anywhere in the world. Carnival is five nights of drinking, dancing, and sensuality, but it is not just a drunken orgy. *Favela* communities prepare all year to produce a spectacular show that parades through Rio's streets. Thousands of elaborately costumed dancers and musicians, in carefully choreographed and rehearsed "samba schools," compete for prizes and prestige.

Even the spontaneous and cruder elements (cross-dressing, water fights) express the urban poor's creative reaction to a society that for the rest of the year ignores them, when it isn't exploiting them. Carnival is a **festival of reversal,** during which the poor take over the streets, dress in fancy clothes, and insist on being heard (Scheper-Hughes 1992; Matta 1993). It is this Carnival of the poor that millions of international tourists pay to see, not the Carnival of the wealthy that takes place behind closed doors in private clubs.

The Brazilian poor are not saints; they exhibit all the ordinary human failures and weaknesses of any other group of people. What is amazing, though, is what they have accomplished with so few resources that mere survival is a daily struggle.

THE HARM OF A MYTH

Marginality is nothing but a terrible distortion of reality, but it has devastating consequences for the poor. To anyone who has not lived with such a powerful stigma, it is hard to imagine the damage that it does. Many of my neighbors in Caranguejo struggled with crippling feelings of inferiority and inadequacy. Even those who have retained a strong sense of self feel pressure to hide their intelligence and personality when interacting with upper-class Brazilians so as not be viewed as dangerous, uppity troublemakers.

Because they are "only *marginais*," they often are treated with unconscious disrespect, as if they don't have feelings or experience pain. Many women in Caranguejo work in upper-class homes as maids and cooks and speak bitterly about their treatment. Even dignified grandmothers are treated as children, watched carefully, and punished for the slightest infraction. For example, many employers fear that the cook intentionally will prepare extra food so that she can eat it or take it home. To prevent this, cooks often are not allowed to eat any of the food that they prepare for the family; leftovers are given to the dog, but not to the cook or her children.

The psychological assaults are destructive, but even more threatening is the physical danger they face because their lives are not highly valued. Not viewed as fully human, their lives, literally, are cheap. This disregard is constantly communicated, from the motorist who accelerates as they cross the street to the policemen who execute their children for crimes real or imagined.

One symptom of these pressures is the complaint of being *aperreado*—so nervous, tense, anxious, or stressed that one is overcome by passivity and trembling. There is also an underlying anger at a world that appears implacably hostile. Because there is no way out, though, the anger is ultimately frustrating (Scheper-Huges 1992). When these nervous attacks hit, my neighbors would rant against a world that seemed determined to break them. Listening to them, I would be left shaken, powerless. Knowing that I could escape the *favela* whenever I wanted but that my neighbors were trapped, I couldn't imagine how they generated the courage to face another day. Amazingly, they did. Brazilian author Jorge Amado in the novel *Shepherds of the Night* described the resilience and humanity of *marginais* in Salvador, Bahia:

> a poor person does more than should be expected . . . just by living, living in the face of such wretchedness. . . And not just satisfied with living, they even lived happily. . . They confronted misery with gaiety. . . They resisted everything; they stood up to life, and they did not live it naked and cold. They dressed it in laughter and music, in human warmth, in courtesy, in that civilization of the Bahian people (1966: 326).

DANGEROUS CITIES

When I lived in Caranguejo (1980–83), the *favela* felt like a safe place. The only time I had anything stolen was once when someone cleaned out my refrigerator; other items (a tape recorder and a radio) were left untouched. There was a neighbor known as Luis the Thief, but he lived quietly, only robbing outside the *favela*. The only real danger seemed to be when drunken men became violent or when the police entered the community.

Security was based on the openness of life in the *favela*. Everyone lived in such close proximity that nothing could be hidden. Everyone knew Luis was a thief, but he didn't mess with his neighbors because he needed their protection from the police. Not everyone in the community got along, but people united against outsiders. For example, when strangers came looking for someone, everyone feigned ignorance until they were convinced that the outsiders intended no harm. Security, then, came from knowing that you were surrounded by friends, neighbors, and relatives.

One night, two women burst into my house brandishing big butcher knives. Fortunately they had come to protect me, not to do me in. Some off-duty policemen were looking for Luis and had shot at him as he dove into the water behind my house. The two women feared that if Luis tried to hide in my house I would be caught in the middle of a fight. The next morning, Luis's corpse was floating behind my house. The police arrived after I left to look for a phone to call them; my neighbors again protected me, claiming that I was gone on a trip and had nothing to do with the dead body. Being known and surrounded by people who always knew what was going on created a sense that even if something bad happened, help would arrive quickly.

When I return to Caranguejo now, however, I am constantly warned to be careful, not to be on the streets at night, not to go to certain neighborhoods. These fears are not unfounded; Recife is a more dangerous city. Violent crime rarely occurs within Caranguejo, but residents know that they are at risk whenever they leave the community. Even within Caranguejo, the sense of security has eroded as drug use has increased. In the early 1980s, there was some marijuana use, but the drug of choice was alcohol. Now, hard drugs are increasingly common. Most disturbing is the daily sight of children high on glue.

As in the United States, there is a correlation between drug use and crime. In 1997, I interviewed teenaged boys in Caranguejo. Many of them reported that they used drugs and possessed handguns to protect themselves and to commit crimes to pay for drugs. As the risks grow, gangs have appeared in the city. In Caranguejo, there are no formal gangs yet, but there are fluctuating networks of young males who commit violent crime. Although most of this crime is committed outside the *favela*, residents are anxious as violent scores sometimes are settled within the community.

The increasing crime and violence are caused by a variety of factors. Most first-generation migrants were committed to the traditional moral codes of their rural communities, and whatever the hardships they encountered in the city, they generally experienced urban life as an improvement. Their children, however, grow up in a very different environment with very different expectations. Without their parents' experience of rural deprivation, the second generation only knows the frustration of observing affluent lifestyles they cannot attain. Brazilian television presents a constant barrage of consumer "needs" in its commercials and in its programming depicting upper-class lifestyles. Many of the kids interviewed described their resentment at not having what they see others enjoying.

Young males often grow up with little discipline or structure in their lives. Boys frequently live in fatherless households, so the primary male role models are peers rather than adults. Even when both parents are present, they struggle to sustain the household and often are absent much of the day. By the time they are 10 years old, most boys have dropped out of school and there are few employment opportunities. While girls are required to take care of the house and younger siblings, boys run loose on the streets. Thus, boys spend much of their time unsupervised and with little to keep them usefully occupied.

The outcome, all too often, is violent behavior. One 16-year-old whom I interviewed was M., known as "the terror" because of his violent behavior. M. described how he would leave the house in the morning looking for an excuse to hurt someone so that he could vent his anger. He and his friends, with whom he shared drugs and participated in robberies, never went anywhere unarmed and have shot several people. The police arrested him twice. Rather than put him on trial, they held him in jail and administered beatings to teach him a lesson. The only thing the beatings taught him, however, was greater frustration and anger.

CONCLUSION

Brazilian cities are contradictory. They appear to be a promised land of jobs, conveniences, and entertainment to millions of poor peasants. At the same time, Brazilian cities seem to be degenerating into an abyss of crime, pollution, and poverty. There is some truth to both views. If there was no reason to believe that life would be better in the city, the rural population would have migrated in greater numbers to the Amazon than to the cities. Urban migration, however, has exaggerated a multitude of social problems.

Brazilian cities are still growing, but the surge has slowed. Migrants are diversifying their destinations, reducing the pressure on a few megacities like Rio and São Paulo. There is no end in sight to migration, however, as mechanization continues to reduce rural employment. Unless land reform is implemented to provide land to rural families, the rural population will have little choice but to migrate either to the cities or to the Amazon. Neither choice is ideal, but for now most migrants prefer the cities despite all their problems. The Brazilian government, though, would prefer that they relocated to Amazonia, where the negative ecological consequences will not be felt as rapidly as the social consequences in the city.

CHAPTER 7

Gender and Family in Brazil

One evening I was eating dinner with a friend in Recife when we heard loud shouts from outside. We ran to the door and saw two angry men facing each another in the middle of the street, just like a Hollywood western. The showdown looked highly unequal. One man, wearing a night watchman's uniform, had a revolver in the holster on his hip while the other man had only a large knife in his hand. Obviously, the man with the gun could shoot his opponent before the knife could put him in any danger.

The man with the knife realized his predicament; the fear was apparent in his voice. He did not back down, though, but held his ground. As the argument came to a climax, the man with the knife pounded his chest with his free hand and roared: "*Sou macho. Sou macho. Pode me matar, mas sou macho!*"— "I'm a man. I'm a man. You can kill me, but I'm a man!" The tremble in his voice made it obvious that he didn't want to die, but he was determined to risk death rather than run away.

This confrontation shows the power of **gender ideologies,** the cultural norms about how men and women should behave. The man with the knife acted as if it were better to die as a "man" (someone who is not a coward) than to survive by running, because then he would cease to be a man. He didn't want to die, but he had been taught that men cannot refuse a challenge to fight. Better to die a man than to endure the shame of running away.

TRADITIONAL GENDER IDEOLOGIES

The traditional gender ideologies in Brazil are called *machismo* and *marianismo* by sociologists (Stevens 1973; Neuhouser 1998). Most Brazilians, though, would be unfamiliar with these terms. Girls and boys are not consciously taught these ideologies, but, like small sociologists, absorb them by observing their social worlds. From birth, boys and girls are treated differently and therefore quickly learn to behave differently. Sociologists have observed the resulting patterns of behavior and the gendered **norms** that guide them and named them *machismo* and *marianismo*. Although these traditional ideologies are powerful and constrain behavior, individuals can rebel against or creatively reshape these gendered expectations.

Machismo

Machismo comes from the root word *macho;* a common word in English as well as Portuguese. In Brazil, *macho* may refer to any male, but usually it indicates a particular kind of man, one who is powerful, fearless, always ready to prove his manhood. In relations with women, he is to be dominant and sexually aggressive. In fact, men are viewed as essentially driven by their biological nature. On one occasion, I was lectured by a Brazilian grandmother on how men get physically ill (headaches, tremors, sleeplessness) if they are foolish enough to abstain from sexual intercourse.

Machismo also defines a gendered **division of labor.** Men are to be active in the **public sphere** of paid labor and politics. The *rua* (street) is a male sphere where men are free to roam. Within the household, men's primary duty is to financially care for the family. The male ideal of sexual promiscuity, however, means this responsibility may extend to several families.

Marianismo

The term *marianismo* refers to Mary the mother of Jesus. Women should imitate Mary's sexual purity and submission to a life of sorrow. Like Mary, Brazilian women are defined by motherhood; their primary duty is **reproductive labor** within the household, taking care of others. Thus, women's primary activities are in the **private sphere,** or **domestic sphere,** within the safety of the *casa* (home). Table 7–1 shows the differences in Brazilian gender ideologies.

Brazilian women appear disadvantaged by these ideologies. Excluded from resources and activities that would give them public power (income, political office), they often are dependent on men to protect and provide for them. Sometimes, dependence forces women to endure abusive situations to gain the resources they and their children need to survive. This is similar in some respects to the traditional gender ideologies in our own culture.

There are important differences, however, between Brazilian and American gender ideologies. For example, in Brazil men are viewed as biologically driven, whereas women are not; the grandmother I mentioned earlier went on to explain that although men cannot live without sex, women can do so quite well. In Brazil women are viewed as more spiritual than men, more moral, and therefore more wise. Men are childlike,

TABLE 7-1

Brazilian Gender Ideologies

Machismo	Marianismo
Aggressive	Passive
Dominant	Submissive
Biological	Spiritual
Physical	Moral
Childlike	Wise
Sexual	Asexual
Political	Apolitical
Public sphere	Private sphere
Rua/street	*Casa*/home
Productive labor	Reproductive labor
Household finances	Household nurture

needing a woman's moral guidance to control their impulsiveness. Thus, women may exercise considerable moral authority over men (especially mothers over sons).

The 16th century priest Antônio Vieira reportedly taught that "a woman should only leave her home three times in her life—when she was baptized, married, and buried" (Silva 1997a: 103). The home, however, can be an important resource and a basis for some power. In Brazil, married women are called *dona*, short for *dona de casa* (owner/mistress of the house), acknowledging female control and expertise. The significance of being a *dona* varies by class. In the upper class, she is responsible for child care and maintenance of the house; she has the authority to manage the household staff, which minimally includes one maid, but also may include a cook, a nanny, and a gardener. Despite the wife's title of *dona de casa*, however, the husband probably holds the actual legal title to the house. Among my neighbors in Caranguejo, though, no one has legal title to the house. In the context of urban poverty, then, the cultural understanding of women as *dona de casa* is used by some women to claim and retain possession of the house if the couple split up.

DOING GENDER

Gender ideologies are like scripts that women and men learn to guide behavior. Those who follow the cultural script closely are praised for **doing gender** well; but if they deviate too far from the script, they will be criticized or even punished. The script, however, only outlines the action in very general terms so that we sometimes are forced to improvise, waiting to see how well we've done by the audience's response. Thus, actual behavior may deviate from the gender ideologies.

For example, *machismo* defines politics as a male sphere, and in fact, most politicians in Brazil are men. In 1994, of the 22 federal ministers only 1 was a woman, and women held only 6 percent of the congressional seats (UN 1995). Thus, when I began my research on grassroots political mobilization in Caranguejo I fully expected men to be the primary community activists. I couldn't have been more wrong.

According to local residents, there have been six major periods of community mobilization since 1971. In only one case were men the chief participants, and that was the least successful mobilization. Women were the founding mothers of the community, having led the initial canal invasion. Women had been so aggressive in their defense of the invasion that a policeman referred to one of the leaders, Dona Nenê, as "worse than a man!" In the following years, women were largely responsible for bringing water, electricity, and a health post to the community (Neuhouser 1995).

Thus, I was confronted with three questions: (1) What was the motivation for women to behave in ways that seemed to defy the ideology of *marianismo*? (2) How had women gotten away with breaking the gender stereotypes? (3) Why didn't men follow their gender script to be more politically active than women?

A Good Mother

The answer to the first question turned out to be quite simple. Women were motivated by motherhood to mobilize in order to access the resources they needed to care for their children. The women who invaded the canal bank were faced with being evicted from their rented rooms. This would have been disastrous. Edeleuza described it this way:

> If I were to be alone with these kids and nowhere to put our heads . . . what would become of me? I would abandon my children? I couldn't. But I have my little house. If I had abandoned my children, today they would say, "I won't even care about my mother; she abandoned me when I was little." Isn't that right?

To *be* a mother, Edeleuza needed a house so that she could keep her children with her; on the street, the family likely would have split up to survive. Thus, for Edeleuza and the other women who invaded and defeated the police effort to remove them, the motivation was maternal not political.

This distinction between maternal and political provides a clue to answering the second question. The women were not viewed as acting deviantly, because they were being good mothers; they simply were taking care of their children. Thus, **deviance** is not necessarily defined by the behavior but by the motivation behind the behavior. For example, despite the gender stereotype that a woman's place is in the home, most poor women are employed. These women are not considered deviant,

Women in the dry sertão *region of northeast Brazil demonstrate the beautiful lace they have made together. In the gender division of labor, lace making is a skill women take great pride in and use to supplement family income.*

however, because they are good mothers, earning income for their children. Wealthy women who work for other reasons (e.g., personal fulfillment) may not be viewed so sympathetically.

Gender Deviance

Surprisingly, there is more leniency for women to act like men than for men to act like women. Women are able to claim that male behavior is necessary to fulfill the requirements of motherhood. Women also may be respected for acting in the more valued *macho* ways. One evening I was watching TV with some friends in the *favela* when I was startled by shouting and the sound of objects smashing that could be heard clearly through the thin walls. My friends were undisturbed by the commotion, continuing to watch TV. When I expressed concern, they laughed and said that the husband must have come home drunk again and his wife and daughter were teaching him a lesson. These two women were deviating wildly from their gender script, but their courage and aggressiveness were admired. A woman like this is known as a *mulher brava*—a brave, wild, fierce woman—and is grudgingly respected for being *macho*.

Because female behavior is less valued, however, male deviance from the gender norms is more likely to be punished. A man who engages in female behavior, like doing the dishes or washing clothes, is ridiculed as a *mulherinha*, a "little woman." In my interviews in Caranguejo, men and women claim that the most deviant act a man can engage in is to be gay. In Brazil, *gay* refers to the passive, feminine partner in homosexual intercourse; the aggressive, masculine partner is not considered gay. Thus, to be gay is to act like a woman and is the least *macho* behavior imaginable. As Edivaldo explained to me, "It is better to be drunk and unemployed than to be gay." Homosexuality for women is not viewed as negatively because the community recognizes that lesbians can be good mothers, and that, after all, is the most important quality in a woman. According to a northeastern folk saying, "if you want to know what kind of woman she is, put a child in her arms" (Souto Maior 1994: 37).

Gender Role Identities

If women in Caranguejo could act politically despite gender norms against it, why were the men so inactive when gender norms approved male political activity? While women acted politically because of their commitment to motherhood, it appears that men were inactive because of their lack of commitment to fatherhood. Activism was dangerous during the military dictatorship, so only those willing to run high risks participated. Women in Caranguejo ran those risks because there was nothing worse for them than to fail to be mothers. Men, however, were less committed to fatherhood because there were other **gender-role identities** available to them.

The primary **gender role** for the man in a household is to provide income for the family. According to Regi, men must take "responsibility for the household, make sure that nothing is lacking," but high unemployment in Caranguejo makes it difficult for men to be good fathers according to the cultural script. Rather than seek other means like the women do to be good parents, many men opt for other roles embedded in the *machista* ideology. Thus, in Caranguejo, "real" men were defined more by sexual promiscuity, playing soccer, fighting, and drinking than by being good fathers (Neuhouser 1998).

GENDER IN THE FAMILY

Among the Brazilian urban poor, male commitment to their **family of procreation** (wife and children) is often tenuous. On the one hand, *machismo* tells men that their primary role is as the family breadwinner, but the economy makes it difficult to find the employment needed to fill that role. (Remember Gilson in Chapter 4, who was so desperate that he worked without pay for a month in hopes of gaining employment.) On the other hand, *machismo* tells men that they should be sexually promiscuous, which often divides their commitment between several households.

Female-Headed Households

Frequently the result among the urban poor is male abandonment of the household. Maria José, who lived across the street from us in Caranguejo, gave birth to 10 children, but the first 7 died. After the next 3 survived, her husband announced that he couldn't support so many kids and left. Maria José, who couldn't read or write, took any work she could find to feed her children. By default, she violated the traditional gender norm by becoming a female head of household. Maria José was hardly alone, however. In 1970, 13 percent of all households were female-headed, but by 1990, 20 percent (7 million) were estimated to be headed by women—(*Veja* 1994; IBGE 1995; UN 1995). The rate is even higher among the urban poor. Recife, the poorest Brazilian city, has the highest percentage of **female-headed households,** 27 percent (*Veja* 1994); in many poor communities like Caranguejo, male-headed households actually may be the minority.

A woman-headed household does not mean that adult men are completely absent, only that weak commitment makes their presence irregular. The stable household nucleus is the mother and her children. In Caranguejo, many female-headed households are multigenerational and **matrilineal** extended families. In other words, the household is composed of several generations of mothers and daughters with their children (grandmother, daughters, grandchildren). Males are present as sons and spouses, but they are more likely to leave and join separate households than are female household members.

There is a disjuncture between **ideal culture** (how people are supposed to behave) and **real culture** (actual behavior). In poor urban communities, female-headed households now are so numerous as to constitute a new norm. Employment as domestic workers is poorly paid, but it allows single mothers to provide for their families. Among the middle- and upper-class households divorce is increasingly common, but the ideal is still a married couple. Because middle- and upper-class men have access to secure, well-paid employment, they can fulfill the traditional role as family provider. In rural areas, women often are dependent on men's income and female-headed households remain rare. Thus, men's ability to conform to *machismo* is impacted by their economic situation. Poor urban men often are criticized for abandoning wives and children, yet in Caranguejo the few men with full-time employment generally were committed to their families.

Women in female-headed households are disadvantaged in many ways. Reliance on a single adult's income means that female-headed households are more likely to fall below the poverty line. Single mothers do all the reproductive labor (housework, child care) and all of the productive labor (paid work). A single mother of seven, Edeleuza described her typical day to me:

> Up by 5:00 AM, she washes the family's clothes by hand so they can dry while she is at work (without washers or driers and with few changes of

clothes, washing and ironing clothes is a daily task). Edeleuza fixes her children's breakfast and lunch, so they won't have to light the gas stove. She then walks to the home where she works, washing, cooking, and cleaning for someone else. In the late afternoon, she runs to pick up the younger kids at the day care center before it closes. Back at home, she begins again—cleaning her own house and cooking dinner. In the evening, the kids must be bathed and put to bed and maybe, in between ironing and starting the next day's meals, she watches some TV before going to bed herself.

Despite the hardships, women may experience certain advantages as a household head in Caranguejo. Employed with her own house, she has an independence that may give her more equality in relationships with men than occurs in many middle- and upper-class families. One day I heard a commotion on the street in front of my house. A woman was brandishing a large knife in her partner's face, letting him know in no uncertain terms that he should leave for good and the quicker the better. He tried to change her mind, but the knife made it clear that it wasn't about to happen. A dramatic breakup, but it certainly wasn't the only time that a woman I knew had the power to end a relationship on her own terms. Employment and possession of the house give many poor urban women the independence to stay in relationships only as long as they find them beneficial.

Independence for women in Caranguejo, however, comes at the cost of poverty and years of hard, unappreciated work. Thus, many single mothers long for a traditional family with a husband responsible for household income. Because domestic service (which most employed women do) is even less valued than the same work done at home, quitting the workforce is a dream of many poor single mothers. Given the strength and self-confidence that they have earned through years of independent struggle, though, it is not clear how well they would readjust to dependence on a man.

RAISING GENDERED CHILDREN

Single mothers in Caranguejo were strong, powerful women who seemed to defy almost every gender norm except motherhood, yet they complained bitterly about men's lack of family commitment. They wanted husbands committed enough, not just to provide income, but also to help with the kids and the housework—changing diapers, washing dishes, and doing laundry. I was curious, then, to observe that daughters were obliged to do housework while sons were rarely asked to help. It seemed that mothers were raising their sons and daughters to repeat the male–female relationships about which the mothers complained so bitterly.

From the time they are small, girls are socialized to become mothers. Women lovingly call baby girls *mãeinha* (little mother or mommy), the same name girls use for their mothers. In this way, girls learn that they are simply smaller versions of their own mothers. Girls are taught to do everything mothers do: cook the rice and beans, wash the clothes by hand, take care of younger brothers and sisters. Boys, though, are free to play on the street with friends, going home only to eat or sleep.

When asked why they raised their children this way, women give a simple answer: They don't want their sons to be gay. They believe that homosexuality is caused by **socialization** not biology; women thought that if they made their sons act like women, they would become gay. Boys who did girls' work would be made fun of, and the ridicule eventually would become a self-fulfilling prophecy. How could any good mother want that for her son? Mothers in Caranguejo often express concern if a teenaged son is not sexually active, less worried about the consequences of promiscuous, usually unprotected, sex than the possibility that he is gay. Ironically, women, as the primary caregivers, socialize children into gender roles that they themselves resent.

THE BRAZILIAN FAMILY

Despite the strains on the Brazilian family, it remains the fundamental social unit. Brazilians' primary allegiance is to their **family of orientation,** or family of birth. Historically, the larger the family the better. In the context of a weak state and unstable economy, large families provide security because kin are supposed to care for and protect one another.

Families often are expanded by **fictive kinship** in which outsiders are treated as kin. The most common form is the godparent system of *compadres* and *comadres.* In the Brazilian Catholic tradition, godparents are chosen to sponsor a child's baptism, establishing a special relationship of intimacy and responsibility, not only between godparents and child, but also between parents and godparents. In effect, it is a way to choose new family members. Family members also can be added through the less formal *agregado* (aggregated) method. *Agregados* live with and are treated as family members. Historically, powerful *fazendeiros* attracted numerous *agregados* dependent on the landowner's generosity. Currently, it provides an informal adoption system to take care of children without parents.

This practice illustrates how much children, even nonkin, are valued in Brazil. Newborns are doted over, dressed in fancy clothes (especially girls), and delightfully caressed cheek to cheek with the phrase *me dá um cheiro,* "give me a smell." Children are often treated permissively by U.S. standards, allowed to stay up late and even given sips of wine or beer. As a result, Brazilian children may appear more at ease interacting with adults than do American children. Birthdays are huge family celebrations, with the entire extended family present to eat, drink, dance, and talk into the early morning hours.

The mother, even when the father is present, is the emotional center of the family, still playing an important role in the lives of married children. The kinship group is extremely important through the entire life course; older children live with relatives if they attend school in another city, and their first jobs may be provided by kin. In an individualistic culture like that in the United States, tight family relations may appear constraining, but in the Brazilian context, where resources often are scarce, families that stick together are more likely to prosper.

CHANGING GENDERED OUTCOMES

Brazilian culture is changing radically; the traditional gender ideologies of *machismo* and *marianismo* increasingly are questioned and transformed, especially by women. The responses to two national surveys (1967 and 1994) reveal dramatic changes. Women were asked if being a wife/mother/housewife was enough to be completely fulfilled; in 1967, 81 percent said yes, but in 1994, 79 percent said no. They also were asked if a woman should work if she doesn't need the income; 68 percent of the women in 1967 said no, but 86 percent said yes in 1994 (*Veja* 1994).

Emergence of Women's Movements

In the years between 1967 and 1994, a dynamic collection of women's movements emerged, articulating old grievances and stimulating new demands (Alvarez 1990). As a result, Brazilian women today are much less likely to conform to the gendered norms of *marianismo* than were their mothers and grandmothers.

During the early 1960s, inflation drastically eroded the earning power of working-class men. As a result, women entered the workforce in unprecedented numbers to help sustain their households. From 1950 to 1970, the proportion of female workers rose from 14 percent to 21 percent (Alvarez 1990). By 1993, 40 percent of the paid labor force was female and 50 percent of all women 10 years and older were working (IBGE 1995).

Women discovered that the gendered division of labor in the home had followed them into the workplace as the jobs available to them were primarily in the service sector. In 1970, 36 percent of the women in the workforce were service workers, compared to just 4 percent of men (SALA 1989). The 1980 census revealed that the most common female job was maid (20 percent), followed by secretaries (15 percent), teachers (8 percent), sales (5 percent), and nurses (3 percent). Thus, over half of all working women were in just five "female" occupations (*Veja* 1994).

Brazilian women, especially dark-skinned women, are relegated to the bottom rungs of the gendered labor market. Women exercise little economic power; only 2 percent of the country's top executives are women. Women workers also earn less than men. In 1990, working women earned on average only 57 percent of what working men earned (*Veja* 1994). Women are 2.5 times more likely than men to earn half a

minimum wage or less, but men are 2.5 times more likely to earn 20 minimum wages or more per month (Bruschini 1994). The gap has narrowed
over the last few decades, but there is still a long way to go.

Brazilian women also found that paid labor did not signify an end to
the domestic division of labor. They were still responsible for the housework: cooking, cleaning, and caring for the family. Working women too
poor to afford a maid of their own faced a **double day** with two jobs—an
ill-paid one outside the home and an unpaid one inside the home. Thus,
entering the workforce increased many women's experience of discrimination and frustration with traditional gender ideologies. As a result,
Brazilian women organized themselves in a wide variety of **women's
movements** that profoundly changed Brazilian society. Women struggled
with an amazing variety of concerns—land, race, inflation, sexuality, birth
control—but their efforts can be grouped into two broad types of movements, feminine and feminist (Alvarez 1990).

Feminine Movements

Feminine movements are organized by women to access the resources
that they need to be good mothers. Participants generally are poor, and
their concerns are very pragmatic, demanding everything from day care
centers for working mothers to clean water and electricity for the home.
Unable to pay for these services, they insisted that the government support their efforts to care for their children. Although based on the traditional maternal gender role, participants indirectly challenged male
power by organizing and entering the political sphere. The mobilizations
in Caranguejo exemplify this pattern.

Feminist Movements

Feminist movements directly challenged male dominance. Primarily
composed of middle- and upper-class women who didn't need governmental help to be mothers, feminist movements confronted issues of inequality and power. Feminists achieved important legal changes in the
treatment of women. The 1988 constitution, for the first time, outlawed
discrimination against women, required equal pay for equal work, and
guaranteed 120 days' maternity leave (Silva 1997a: 114). Although en-
forcement of these rights remains sporadic, women now have a legal
basis for their struggle for equality. Feminist concerns, however, extended into cultural spheres that law alone couldn't transform. Feminists
pushed for changes in the basic perception of women and their social
roles by organizing conferences, publishing magazines, and producing
plays and movies.

One critical issue raised by feminists was violence against women,
which historically had been legally tolerated under the principles of "violent emotion" and "defense of honor." Male violence was excused if

the woman provoked the man to violent emotion; if the woman sexually betrayed a husband or boyfriend, even murder was permitted in defense of male honor. In 1979, however, when Raúl Doca Street was sentenced to just two years for killing his lover after she attempted to end their relationship, thousands of women protested outside the courthouse and the sentence on appeal was increased to 15 years. In 1991, the Brazilian Supreme Court finally ruled that the defense of honor principle was illegitimate though it continues to be used in some low-profile cases (Nelson 1996).

Women's Police Stations

Perhaps the most innovative feminist strategy to reduce violence against women was the creation of the first women's police stations—*delegacias da mulher* (DDMs)—in the world. DDMs are entirely staffed by female police officers who investigate crimes against women. Feminists hoped that female victims would be more likely to report crimes to female officers and that female officers would be more motivated to investigate and prosecute these crimes. The first DDM opened in São Paulo in 1985 and received approximately 12,000 complaints in the first two years, over 40 percent of which resulted in prosecutions. DDMs quickly proliferated; by 1993, there were 185 throughout Brazil receiving over 12,000 complaints every month. There has been criticism that the DDMs have performed no better than traditional police stations, but at the very least, the DDMs and feminist denunciations have forced recognition that violence against women is a significant social problem (Corral 1993; Saffioti 1994; Nelson 1996).

Women and Democracy

Despite the variety of concerns and the fundamental differences in feminine and feminist movements, participants were staunchly prodemocracy. The military dictatorship was viewed as a barrier to attaining any of their goals, while democratic rights and processes could facilitate their struggles. Thus, women's organizations were at the forefront of the democratization movement in the 1970s and early 1980s that helped end 25 years of dictatorship (Alvarez 1990). In the years since, women's organizations have struggled to make democracy a reality by pressuring the government to *act* democratically by responding to the needs of Brazilian women, most of whom are economically and racially disadvantaged.

FERTILITY: A DEMOGRAPHIC REVOLUTION

Twenty years ago, demographers predicted that Brazil would have a population of 190 million people by the mid-1990s. They only missed it by about 30 million too many. They were so far off because, without anyone noticing, Brazilian women carried out a women's revolution, claiming control of their own fertility (Pinheiro 1997). Against explicit Catholic teaching and virtually without men's help, Brazilian women drastically cut the growth rate because they decided to have fewer children.

Until 1940, Brazil had a relatively high fertility rate, but because the mortality rate also was high, population growth was moderate at just under 2 percent a year (see Figure 7–1). After 1940, however, the mortality rate dropped rapidly while fertility remained high; as late as 1960–65, the average woman gave birth to 6.2 babies during her lifetime. Population growth accelerated by 50 percent to almost 3 percent annually during the 1960s and 1970s, a **natural increase** due to the combination of lower mortality and high fertility. This is the period when demographers made dire predictions about a population explosion. Unexpectedly, by 1990 Brazilian women had cut their fertility almost in half. Today, the average woman has only 3.5 births during her lifetime, and the population growth rate during the early 1990s was only 1.6 percent, the lowest rate since the late 1800s (SALA 1989; UN 1995; Coelho 1996).

Brazilian women want fewer children. According to the National Demographic and Health Survey, 40 percent of the women with one child and 84 percent of the women with two don't plan on having another; 94 percent of the women with three children say they are done (Pinheiro 1997). Although motherhood continues to be the norm for Brazilian women, as **infant mortality** falls and women increasingly work outside the home, the number of children women desire has dropped.

FIGURE 7–1

Demographic Changes in Brazil, 1872–1995

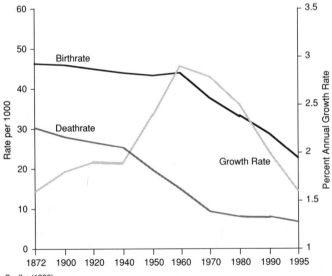

Source: Coelho (1996).

Brazilian women didn't just want fewer children; they made it happen. Of all women age 15 to 49, 27 percent have had tubal ligations; for cohabiting women the figure is 40 percent. Although many women chose sterilization, there are concerns that it is sometimes pushed on women, especially if they are poor and black (Alvarez 1990). For example, Benedita da Silva (1997a: 112–13), the first black female senator in Brazilian history, notes that the World Bank provided $600 million to set up family-planning clinics in seven of the poorest states that have been accused of failing to provide women with options, urging women as young as 13 to accept sterilization. As Benedita points out, "[t]here is a big difference between family planning and population control"; the first gives women the power to make choices, whereas the second is the power to deny choices to women.

An estimated one million illegal abortions are performed each year in Brazil (Pinheiro 1997). Abortions have declined, however, as other forms of birth control have become more available. According to the 1986 National Survey on Maternal-Infant Health and Family Planning (PNSMIPF), the pill is the second most common form of birth control after tubal ligations, taken by 25 percent of women age 15 to 44. Only 4.3 percent of the women used the rhythm method (abstinence during periods of heightened fertility), the only method accepted by the Catholic Church. In all, 66 percent of cohabiting Brazilian women in this age group were using some form of birth control (Carranza 1994).

In contrast to women's determination to reduce fertility, men have done very little. Only about 2 percent of Brazilian men have had vasectomies (Pinheiro 1997). Condom use has increased, especially among young males, but more to prevent disease (fear of AIDS) than to help their sexual partners avoid pregnancies. Even so, condom use remains quite low in Brazil; according to the PNSMIPF survey, only 1.7 percent of cohabiting women age 15 to 44 had partners using condoms (Carranza 1994).

WOMEN AND EDUCATION

Education may be the most critical long-term determinant of women's status, impacting every area of life. Without education, women are unable to compete for good jobs and better wages; women without any schooling are 32 percent less likely to use birth control than women who have completed primary school (Carranza 1994: 129). If educational equality is a prerequisite for gender equality, then there is reason for hope because Brazil has made great progress in this area.

In 1879, coeducation was mandated for Brazil's public schools; at the same time, universities were opened to women. Progress was slow, however. Because it was improper for girls to be taught by men, their enrollment could expand only to the extent that women were trained as teachers. As a result, girls' education continued to lag behind that of boys. In 1890, only 10 percent of the women were literate, compared to 19 percent of the men. Even when women succeeded in entering college, they did not receive the same education as men. For example, in 1940 the most common advanced degrees for men were in law and medicine; for women the most common degree was in music (Besse 1996).

Although progress was slow, it did come. By 1970, there were virtually as many girls as boys enrolled in school, primary through university. Young women (age 15–24) actually had a slightly higher literacy rate than their male peers, 75 percent to 74 percent (UN 1991). By 1990, the literacy rate for women (age 15–24) had risen to 91 percent, whereas men, at 85 percent, had failed to keep up. At the university level, there are now 110 women enrolled for every 100 men. Although some fields remain gender stereotyped—in 1990, 80 percent of education majors were women, but only 17 percent of engineering majors were women—other stereotypes have broken down; for instance, women were 44 percent of the law students and 64 percent of the medical students (SALA 1996: 249). Perhaps most striking is that 41 percent of university professors were women in 1990, compared to just 27 percent in the United States (UN 1995).

Education, however, is not available to all women. Brazil is a highly stratified society, and access to schooling is constrained by race and class. Despite rapidly expanding enrollment, only 5 percent of all women 18 to 24 attended university in 1980 (Alvarez 1990). The combination of few university openings and the generally poor quality of public education in Brazil means that affluent students from expensive private schools are much better prepared to pass the university entrance exam. With few poor women able to enter college, higher education fails to serve as a major avenue of upper mobility. Thus, white women in Brazil are four times more likely than black women to have some university education; as a result, just 2 percent of working black women are in prestigious professions like law, medicine, or engineering (Alvarez 1990).

CONCLUSION

The traditional Brazilian gender ideologies—*machismo* and *marianismo*—divide the world into male and female spheres. Men are expected to be active in the public sphere of work and politics; women are directed to the private sphere of home and family. Exclusion from the public sphere would seem to disadvantage women, denying them access to valuable resources, yet women as mothers may exercise a significant amount of power in relationships with male family members.

These gender ideologies currently are being challenged and transformed. Women's involvement in education, the labor force, and politics has increased rapidly in the last three decades. Women are claiming new roles in Brazilian society. Although women have fewer children today, motherhood and family remain central to most women's lives. Shrinking family size has not meant a decline in the social importance of the family, as it continues to be the fundamental social group in Brazil.

CHAPTER 8

Religion in Brazil

In northeast Brazil, St. John's Day is among the most traditional and popular holidays in the year. It occurs in June. Women prepare numerous dishes from the fresh corn then being harvested. Children perform a traditional play, a "hillbilly" shotgun wedding that everyone loves despite the familiar ending. Large bonfires are central to the festivities. Neighbors join in circle dances around the fires and roast ears of corn. For weeks, families collect wood, stacking it higher and higher. Then on St. John's eve, the bonfires are lit, illuminating the night with flying sparks and filling the air with smoke and ash.

Curious why bonfires are linked to the celebration of St. John's Day, I asked a neighbor. He was surprised that I didn't know my Bible well enough to answer the question myself. He explained that John the Baptist's mother had set a bonfire on a hilltop to signal Mary (the expectant mother of Jesus) that John was born. A wonderful story, but it's not in the Bible.

St. John's Day celebrations illustrate several important things about religion in Brazil. First, Catholicism has shaped religious practice, especially in the veneration of saints. Second, Brazilians are very religious; it is the rare person that does not believe in the reality of a spiritual world inhabited by supernatural beings who interact with us. Third, although most Brazilians identify themselves as Catholic, the church's influence is more widespread than deep. Faced with a chronic shortage of priests, the church struggled to socialize the population into orthodox Catholicism. Thus, most Brazilians practice **popular Catholicism,** mixing official teaching with folk beliefs that include elements from other religions.

Although it has the largest Catholic population of any country, characterizing Brazil as the world's most Catholic nation is misleading. Catholicism was the official religion since the Portuguese conquest, but it never has held a monopoly on Brazil's religious imagination, where a bewildering variety of religious beliefs and practices mingle. Indigenous religions predated Catholicism, and African religions arrived soon after.

Today, Protestantism is growing so rapidly that Catholics may soon become the minority in Brazil.

Brazilians are adept at blending the different religious influences, rarely heeding the exhortations of religious leaders to maintain the purity of the faith. Uniquely Brazilian religions have evolved, combining elements of many traditions. In Brazil, not only are boundaries between religions blurred, so is the very line between spiritual and material worlds.

RELIGIOUS COMPLEXITIES

Perhaps no one embodies the complexities of Brazilian religion as well as the Franciscan priest Leonardo Boff. In May 1985, Boff was silenced by the Vatican, ordered to cease all preaching, teaching, and publishing (Berryman 1997). Punishment was in response to the book *Church: Charism and Power* (1985) in which Boff combined Marxist class analysis, suspiciously Protestant ideas about the authority of the church being located in the laity, and a chapter entitled "In Favor of Syncretism" that seemed to open the door to African and indigenous religious influences.

Boff was one of the leading voices of liberation theology, which insisted that the church make a "preferential option for the poor." This required transforming Brazil's exploitative economic and political structures, as well as the hierarchical nature of the Catholic Church itself. If the church truly served the poor by participating in their struggle for economic, political, and spiritual liberation, it was hoped that the rising tide of converts to Protestantism, leftist ideologies, and African spiritism would be stemmed (Neuhouser 1989).

The Vatican in Rome, however, was not as sensitive to the changes occurring in Brazil as it was to fears of communist infiltration, loss of church authority, and **syncretism.** Boff's punishment was intended to halt the spread of these dangerous, perhaps heretical ideas. The strategy backfired, however, as Boff became an "unwilling celebrity" (Smith 1991: 226). Brazilian bishops publicly criticized the Vatican, workers protested by going on strike, and T-shirts were sold depicting a gagged Boff. Finally, in April 1986, Boff's punishment was lifted. Although Boff was allowed to communicate publicly again, the tensions in Brazilian religious practice certainly had not been resolved.

THE HISTORY OF CATHOLICISM IN BRAZIL

From the moment the Portuguese stepped onto the sand of the newly discovered Brazilian coast, they sought to convert the indigenous peoples to Catholicism. The Brazilian church, though, was relatively weak, subordinate to the Portuguese crown and financially dependent on the *fazendeiros*. As a result, the church generally supported the political and economic inequality imposed by the Portuguese. The poor were taught to accept their lot in life as God's will, a religious fatalism still frequently expressed in the phrase *se Deus quiser*, "if God wills." Whatever happens is what God wills; it is beyond human control.

Not everyone in the church, however, supported Portuguese colonial policies. Jesuit priests struggled to protect Indians from enslavement by establishing villages, *aldeias*, that could be defended from Portuguese slavers. The high mortality rate of slaves, however, meant that *fazendeiros* constantly sought replacements and bitterly resented Jesuit interference. In 1759, they finally convinced the crown to expel the Jesuits from Brazil. The *aldeias* were destroyed and their inhabitants abducted into slavery (Burns 1993; Ribeiro 1995).

The single greatest obstacle to effective evangelization was a chronic shortage of priests. Although Mary is the role model for Brazilian women, Jesus never was for men. His celibacy and failure to defend himself was more consistent with feminine norms than with *machismo*. Sexual abstinence was hardly a selling point when Brazilian men considered entering the priesthood. Historically, the church was unable to recruit sufficient priests and has depended heavily on European and North American priests. Even so, at the turn of the century, there was only one priest for every 5,700 Brazilians, and by 1990 this number had more than doubled to one priest for every 10,500 (see Figure 8–1; SALA 1996). Thus, there are many communities, especially in rural areas, where the arrival of a priest is a yearly event when 12 months' worth of baptisms and weddings take place.

FIGURE 8–1

Number of People per Catholic Priest

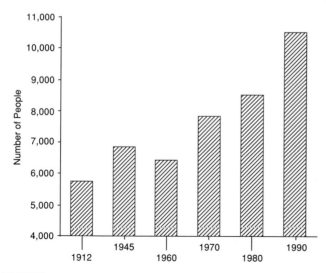

Source: SALA (1996).

POPULAR CATHOLICISM

With so few priests, most Brazilian Catholics receive little religious instruction. Thus, everyday Catholic beliefs and practices often have little to do with the doctrines and rituals specified by Rome. Outwardly submissive to priests, bishops, and the Pope, Brazilians defined Catholicism in their own way, more as daily interaction with Mary and the saints than as formal religious behaviors like baptism, confession, or mass.

Popular Brazilian Catholicism is pragmatic, seeking solutions to everyday problems. In their hour of need, Brazilians solicit help from Mary and the saints. It is a spiritual **patron–client system**, with patron saints assisting clients in exchange for devotion. Individuals may be devotees of any saint, but they seek the one who specializes in their problem. To win favor, they promise some act of devotion, but often they wait to see if their prayers are answered before fulfilling their side of the bargain.

SPIRITISM

Spiritism refers to a variety of religious practices that share belief in supernatural spirits who communicate with humans through the temporary possession of devotees. In rituals, participants open themselves to the spirit world. While the possession lasts, the spirit may speak, dance, or eat, temporarily gaining the use of a physical body.

There are three widespread forms of spiritism—African spiritism, *Kardecismo*, and *Umbanda*—but it is difficult to know how many Brazilians are adherents. For centuries, spiritism was illegal, repressed by the authorities and stigmatized as black magic by the Catholic Church. Only recently have practitioners begun to acknowledge their affiliation in the census and surveys. Many spiritists identify themselves as Catholics, seeing no contradiction between practicing spiritism and participating in the church. In *Shepherds of the Night*, novelist Jorge Amado describes an infant baptism performed by a Catholic priest, but the godfather, chosen by the baby's father, is the African deity *Ogun*. Many Brazilians share the attitude of the baby's father that Catholicism and spiritism "as everyone knows, blend with and understand one another" (Amado 1966: 174).

African Spiritism

African slaves were forcibly baptized and given rudimentary religious instruction, but they continued to practice spiritism despite severe physical punishment. To disguise their rituals, slaves used the names of Catholic saints to refer to African *orixás* (deities). *Ogum*, god of war, became St. George; *Xangô*, god of thunder and lightening, became St. Jerome; *Iemanjá*, the sea goddess, became Mary; and *Exú* became the devil. The Portuguese believed that their slaves were good Catholics, devoted to the saints, when in fact they were honoring *orixás* under saintly aliases. This deception allowed African spiritism to survive in Brazil and created an avenue by which African influences permeated popular Catholicism.

Despite centuries of repression, African spiritism was never eradicated. The most important centers are the urban hubs of the former slave economy, each of which received slightly different tribal influences. Thus, African spiritism is known as *Xangô* in Recife, *Candomblé* in Salvador, and *Macumba* in Rio de Janeiro. There are regional variations in the deities venerated and the ritual forms, but spiritist practice follows a similar pattern everywhere (Brown 1994).

In spiritist ritual, *orixás* are invited to appear and take possession of devotees. The *orixás* are enticed by special foods or sometimes animal sacrifice. Pounding drums call the *orixás* and accompany dancing and singing. The pulsing beat of drums and feet causes devotees to enter a trance in which their bodies are possessed by an *orixá*. The *orixá*, then, can speak directly with those present, offering information or advice.

Because of its origins, African spiritism is associated with the darker-skinned Brazilian poor and is often scorned as a backward and crude religion. In fact, Brazilians of all classes and races believe in the power of the *orixás*; even those unwilling to seek their help respect and fear them. Few are brave or foolish enough to disturb offerings of food or flowers left in public places for the *orixás*. Once I saw an offering placed in the middle of a busy intersection in Recife and was amazed to watch normally heedless drivers carefully swerve to avoid hitting the plate of food.

Kardecism

At the opposite end of the spiritist continuum is *Kardecismo,* named for the druid spirit Allan Kardec, who dictated a series of books to the Frenchman Léon Rivail beginning in 1855. The books combined New Testament ethics, eastern belief in reincarnation, and the science of positivism. *Kardecismo* teaches that the spirits of more highly evolved humans return to offer advice and healing. Communication with spirits is very different than in African spiritism. Without drums, sacrifices, or dancing, a medium simply opens up to the spirit world and enters a trance. Although anyone can communicate with the spirits, not everyone has developed his or her ability. The medium writes down the message dictated by the spirit, which may be general advice or teaching or a private message to a particular person. Some renowned mediums like Chico Xavier receive long lines of people hoping for a personal message from the spirit world. Everything is done quietly and calmly. Classes are offered in the basic tenets of *Kardecismo*, intended to exhort listeners to practice the high ethical standards of evolved spirits.

The focus on writing, reading, and studying messages limits *Kardecismo*'s appeal to the educated sectors of Brazilian society, who, because of racial stratification, tend to be white and concentrated in the more prosperous south and southeast. The spirit guides usually are European or Asian. African and Indian spirits are viewed as less evolved, so *orixás* are less esteemed. Kardecists are renowned for their charity, distributing food, clothes, and milk to the poor (Brown 1994; Hess 1994).

Umbanda

Umbanda is uniquely Brazilian, blending the spirits of Africans, Indians, and *Kardecismo* with Catholic saints. Ritual practices are similar to African spiritism, with possession occurring in the midst of music and dancing, but there are major differences. In the singing, African lyrics are replaced with Portuguese. Rather than *orixás*, *Umbandistas* primarily call on the spirits of humans as in *Kardecismo*, but unlike *Kardecismo*, the spirits are not Europeans, but stereotypical Brazilian *caboclos* (Indians—young, proud, and easily angered) and *pretos velhos* (old blacks—mature, submissive, and wise). *Umbanda* acknowledges other spirits as well, such as African *orixás* like *Xangó* and *Iemanjá,* and the Catholic saints known in Brazil as *Cosmo* and *Damião* (Brown 1994).

Umbanda participants are as varied and representative of Brazil as their beliefs and practices. Leaders usually are more educated and whiter, emphasizing *Kardecist* elements, whereas followers are darker skinned and more influenced by African spiritism. Distinctly Brazilian, its popularity grew rapidly during the nationalistic 1960s and 1970s, but recently the number of adherents has declined. As Brazilians increasingly acknowledge their African origins, many *Umbanda* centers are purifying their rituals of non-African influences (Brown 1994).

PROTESTANTISM

Until the 19th century, Protestants were a trivial presence in Brazil. Immigration was limited to Catholics, so the only Protestants were foreigners—businessmen and embassy staff (with their families) from countries like the United States and England, who the government allowed to build a few Protestant churches and cemeteries. As they rarely attempted to convert Brazilians and their religious services were not conducted in Portuguese, their impact on Brazilian religiosity was minimal.

In the mid-1800s, Protestant missionaries began arriving. The first may have been a Scot named Robert Kakkey, who disembarked in Rio de Janeiro in 1855 to found a congregational church. U.S. Presbyterian missionaries arrived in 1859. This first missionary wave came mostly from traditional denominations like Baptist, Methodist, and Episcopalian. They focused their efforts on the small urban middle class, who appeared most open to Protestantism because of its association with modern ideas of capitalism and individualism (Martin 1989; Page 1995).

A Methodist youth group standing in front of their church, which is still under construction, illustrates the rapid growth of Protestantism in Brazil in recent decades.

During the 19th and early 20th centuries, Protestant growth was slow. **Conversion** required the rejection of important aspects of Brazilian culture, especially for men. Protestants were not allowed to drink, smoke, dance, or play soccer. Rejection of these "vices" is so central to Protestant identity that many times when I've turned down an offer of cigarettes, I am immediately asked, "Are you Protestant?" Conversion also threatened the family, as converts cannot participate in family gatherings that include alcohol or in rituals to become godparents. Thus, Protestantism was viewed not only as a heretical movement but also as a threat to the most fundamental building block of Brazilian society. Antagonism to Protestantism was further heightened by its exclusive claim to followers' allegiance. Unlike the relatively tolerant attitude of popular Catholicism and spiritism, Protestant churches demand that their members renounce participation in all other religions.

To make headway in a hostile environment, early Protestant missionaries founded modern hospitals and schools. Despite sustained missionary effort, Protestantism remained a somewhat foreign enclave in Brazilian society until the mid-20th century. By the 1990s, though, Protestantism had grown so rapidly that currently there are more Protestant pastors than Catholic priests (15,000 to 13,000) and more people attending Protestant worship services than Catholic mass. A conservative estimate indicates that 10 percent of Brazilians are now Protestant; other estimates go as high as 16 percent. If current trends continue, Protestants will be a majority of the population within two generations (Martin 1989; Giles 1992). Figure 8–2 shows the growth in Protestantism in Brazil.

FIGURE 8–2

Protestant Percentage of the Total Population in Brazil

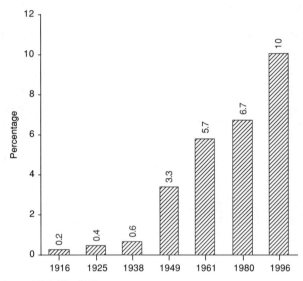

Source: Neuhouser (1989); Giles (1992).

Pentecostalism

The vast majority of this growth occurred outside the traditional denominations supported by foreign missionaries, primarily in locally led Pentecostal churches. Pentecostal churches like the Assemblies of God—the largest denomination in Brazil with 2.9 million members (Barros and Capriglione 1997)—emphasize the empowerment of the Holy Spirit, the primary evidence of which is miraculous feats like speaking in tongues, prophecy, and healing. In 1930 only about 10 percent of Protestants were Pentecostals, but by 1964 they represented between 70 and 80 percent of all Protestants (Martin 1989: 65).

Pentecostals are more Brazilian than earlier forms of Protestants. Pentecostal worship, which bears striking similarities to spiritist practices, focuses on manifestations of the Holy Spirit, which are facilitated through singing repetitive choruses accompanied by rhythmic swaying and clapping. Some churches have bands complete with electric guitars and drums. Most commonly, the Holy Spirit's arrival is announced by speaking in tongues (unknown languages) and miraculous healings.

Pentecostals are growing everywhere, but for several reasons, most rapidly among the urban poor. First, Pentecostal churches provide a new family to isolated city residents, many of whom have left their rural birth families. The kin-like bonds between members are emphasized by calling one another *irmão* and *irmã* (brother and sister). Second, people who are largely powerless within the urban environment are offered power. To those without health care, healing is promised; to those vulnerable to crime and violence, protection and security are promised. Thus, Pentecostalism offers Brazilians an improved social world (a new family and resources) in a way that is believable because it is consistent with folk religious belief in supernatural spirits who intervene in human life.

Cultural Impact

Despite similarities to other Brazilian religions, Pentecostalism embodies several innovations that may provoke important modifications in Brazilian culture. First, historically church and state were so interconnected in Brazil that there was little room for freedom of conscience. There was a single religious and political orthodoxy; any deviations were punished by the combined power of the Catholic Church and the Brazilian government. Pentecostalism establishes a religious sphere in which government has no authority, so for the first time, a significant number of Brazilians are living out the concept of government limited by the free exercise of conscience. Some sociologists believe that in the long run this will stabilize Brazilian democracy (Martin 1989; Smith 1998).

Second, Pentecostalism's rigorous ethical standards require a radical transformation of male behavior that may dramatically impact gender relations. *Machista* culture pushes men to prove their manhood in drinking, fighting, and sexual promiscuity, all of which are prohibited in Pentecostalism. Men are directed to devote themselves and their income to the family, drastically reducing a major source of marital conflict. The pressure on Pentecostal men to revert to *machista* behavior is often intense, but the church provides positive reinforcement and discipline for those who backslide. Elizabeth E. Brusco (1995) argues that conversion implies a "domestication" of men as they turn their attention from the *rua* (street) to the *casa* (home). This may be why Brazilian women are converting at higher rates than men.

LIBERATION THEOLOGY

In the second half of the 20th century, Catholicism's dominant position was eroded by the increasingly open practice of spiritism and rapid Protestant growth. Imported secular ideologies and philosophies like Marxism and positivism also won converts. As a result, the percentage of Brazilians claiming Catholic identity declined; even more alarming to Catholic leaders was an abrupt drop in the number of Catholics actually practicing their faith. One study claimed that from 1900 to 1970 (years during which well over 90 percent of the population was Catholic) the percentage of practicing Catholics in Brazil fell from 80 to 62 percent (SALA 1989).

The Brazilian Catholic church was ill-prepared to respond to competition. Chronically short of priests and with a hierarchical church structure that gave little organizational responsibility to members, the church was unable to stop a steady loss of members. Currently, 500,000 Brazilians convert to Protestantism each year (Tapia 1992). Increasingly, the church's traditional support for the status quo was rejected for religions and ideologies that offered hope and opportunity for improvement. Thus, the Brazilian church found itself in a situation in which holding to traditional practices appeared to condemn it to an increasingly marginal role in society.

The most significant attempt to make the Catholic Church relevant to the changing Brazilian environment was the theology of liberation. Liberation theology was not unique to Brazil, but the Brazilian church provided some of its major figures (Dom Helder Camara, Leonardo Boff) and probably was more deeply affected by its teachings than any other Latin American church (Neuhouser 1989). The fundamental idea in liberation theology is that God is on the side of the poor; therefore the church must defend and support the poor. This was a radical reversal of traditional Catholic teaching in Brazil and provoked the wrath of wealthy Brazilian Catholics, as well as the military regime during the dictatorship (1964–85; Lernoux 1980).

The basic strategy of liberation theology was to empower the poor laity by organizing ecclesiastical base communities (CEBs). In the CEBs, the laity were given tasks that previously had been entrusted only to priests, like teaching and evangelization. CEB members were encouraged to organize and engage in political activities that ranged from demanding government provision of community services to protesting human rights abuses by the military. By the mid-1980s, estimates of the number of functioning CEBs went as high 80,000, with perhaps four million Brazilian Catholics participating (Lernoux 1987).

No one was more closely identified with liberation theology or more responsible for its formation in Brazil than Dom Helder Camara. Appointed archbishop of Recife in the turbulent days following the 1964 military coup, Dom Helder was outspoken in his commitment to justice, mobilizing the Brazilian church to make a "preferential option for the poor." Under the military regime, however, anyone defending the poor ran the risk of being labeled a communist, and even his high church position didn't protect Dom Helder from persecution. From 1968 to 1977, Dom Helder was prohibited from public speaking and Brazilian newspapers could not mention his name. He received numerous death threats, and one of his priests was machine-gunned to death in front of his residence. His courage and commitment, however, inspired many in Brazil and around the world (Kemper and Engel 1987).

During the 1990s, several factors have caused the momentum of liberation theology and the CEBs to fade. First, under the military, the only somewhat protected space for political activists was within the church-sanctioned CEBs. With the end of the dictatorship, many activists shifted their energies into democratic politics, organizing political parties and running for office. Thus, the CEBs lost many of their most motivated and capable leaders. Second, liberation theology drew on Marxist critiques of capitalism to analyze the roots of poverty in Brazil. The collapse of communist regimes in eastern Europe and the Soviet Union seemed to undermine liberation theology's claims. Even if capitalism did create some injustices and cause poverty, there no longer seemed to be any obvious alternative economic system with which to replace it. Third, support or at least tolerance of liberation theology by the Vatican was replaced with papal opposition. Pope John Paul II's experiences in his native Poland made him determined to eradicate liberation theology's influence. In an ironic imitation of the military's treatment of Dom Helder, in 1985 the Vatican silenced the Brazilian priest Leonardo Boff for his writings on liberation theology (Smith 1991: 106).

A more effective strategy against liberation theology has been the replacement of progressive bishops with conservatives. When Dom Helder retired, he was replaced by a conservative, Dom José Cardoso. The new archbishop terminated many of Dom Helder's initiatives, such as *Justiça e Paz* (Justice and Peace—a group of lawyers who provided free legal support to the poor), and closed the seminary with its faculty of liberation theologians.

A symbol of this increasingly divided church is the *Morro da Conceição* (Hill of the Conception) in Recife. The Morro is the highest and most sacred point in the city, topped by a plaza with a church and a statue of Mary. Surrounding it is a large poor neighborhood where for years Padre Reginaldo worked with a very active CEB movement. Dom José clashed with Padre Reginaldo and attempted to remove him from the parish. When the replacement priest arrived, he found Padre Reginaldo locked inside the church with his supporters. The police were called in to break the lock and evict them. Instead of leaving the community as ordered, however, Padre Reginaldo and the CEB rented a house at the opposite end of the plaza from the church and continue to meet. Thus, two Catholic churches compete for the allegiance of those who live on the Hill of the Conception, one known as the "popular church" and the other as the "church of the hierarchy."

CHARISMATIC CATHOLICISM

No one knows what the outcome of the conflict between the conservative and progressive wings of the Catholic church in Brazil will be, but it may be increasingly irrelevant as a new movement has spread within the church, Pentecostalism. Many CEBs have switched from discussing politics to speaking in tongues. Catholic charismatic services are indistinguishable from Pentecostal services except for subtle indicators like references to Mary or the use of a rosary.

The charismatic movement may help stem the flood of Protestant conversions, but it concerns both the conservative and progressive wings of the church. The direct involvement of the Holy Spirit makes conservative bishops and priests uncomfortable because it undermines their authority. Progressives are unhappy because the movement downplays the importance of political activism. Some Catholic leaders, however, recognize that such a widespread movement must be meeting important needs that neither the CEBs nor the hierarchy were meeting.

In 1995, I talked with two nuns who had spent years working with CEBs in northeast Brazil. They were frustrated with the movement's loss of momentum and recognized that Pentecostalism was attracting the poor Brazilians who were expected to be drawn to liberation theology. The nuns observed that the CEB's focus on political and economic problems had worn down participants. The Pentecostals, they concluded, recognized that the poor don't need constant reminding of life's difficulties; what they seek in religion is a release, an experience of joy and power that sustains them through the week. Ultimately, it may be easier for Brazilians to believe their problems will be solved by supernatural intervention than by the suddenly altruistic efforts of Brazilian politicians.

CONCLUSION

Contemporary religious practice in Brazil is a mixture of the religious traditions of the racial groups that make up the population: Indian, European, and African. Despite diverse origins, Brazilian religiosity is characterized by two traits: (1) belief in a spiritual world inhabited by supernatural beings (saints, orixás, Holy Spirit) able and willing to intervene in human affairs, and (2) a pragmatic orientation that seeks to establish patron–client relationships with supernatural beings to solve everyday life problems. For most Brazilians, the ordinary material world is populated with unseen but powerful supernatural forces that must be respected, placated, or avoided.

Religion's historical evolution in Brazil illustrates the dynamic of religious competition. At the conquest, the Catholic Church established a religious monopoly, denying the right to practice alternative religions. A religious monopoly may exercise power widely, but it rarely penetrates deeply (Stark and McCann 1993). If Brazilians become Catholic at birth, then little belief or practice can be required by the church.

The emergence of religious competition in the 20th century revealed the Brazilian church's weak foundations, as millions of Catholics converted or adopted syncretic practices. In response, the church sought new strategies to hold the allegiance of the population. Liberation theology and a reaffirmation of conservative doctrine are alternative visions within Brazilian Catholicism, as the church struggles to respond to this new situation. In the meantime, Catholics in Brazil increasingly are adopting Pentecostal practices within a Catholic framework.

It is not clear how effective these strategies will be. None appears as successful as Pentecostalism. If current trends continue over the next few decades, Protestants will become the majority. Because Catholicism has been so much a part of Brazilian culture and because Brazilians are religiously creative, adopting and combining beliefs and practices in new and unexpected ways, it is hard to imagine what the ramifications of this religious transition might be. Sociologists, however, have identified two possibilities: (1) deemphasis on *machista* gender norms for men, and (2) greater cultural support for democracy.

CHAPTER 9

Brazil in a Globalizing World

This summer (1998) when I return to Brazil, it will mark 25 years since I first stepped off the plane in Campinas, São Paulo, a frightened and very naive 16-year-old. I certainly know more about Brazil now than I did then. Years of sociological study have provided me with facts about Brazil (*saber*) that I had no clue about before I started. Years of living and working in Brazil have provided me with innumerable experiences of the country, its people and culture (*conhecer*).

Every time I return to Brazil for research, though, I see something that I had never noticed before. And I'm shocked that I could have spent so much time and energy getting to know Brazil and yet been oblivious to something that had been right before my eyes all the time. For example, in Chapter 7 I described how I lived for three years in Caranguejo without ever realizing that community mobilization was gendered. This experience is always humbling, but also exhilarating as I realize how much remains to be discovered.

But what does it all mean? Given all the information and experience and analysis, how are we to understand Brazil? In Chapter 1, I introduced two very different interpretations of Brazil. **Modernization theory** suggests that Brazil is modernizing, industrializing, and developing. The transition process is inevitably painful, but the costs today will be worth the future benefits of greater wealth, health, and technology. In the preceding chapters there was evidence that supports such an interpretation. Brazil has industrialized and urbanized. Education is more available; life expectancy has risen and fertility has fallen.

This book has presented other evidence as well, evidence that supports the **dependency** framework. Brazil remains extremely vulnerable to fluctuations in the world economy. Rising interest rates and falling prices for Brazil's exports created a debt crisis and economic recession in the early 1980s. Although foreign loans played an important role in Brazilian development, during the 1980s there was a net outflow of capital from Brazil, as debt repayment exceeded new loans. In fact, Brazil paid foreign banks "twice as much in interest—approximately $105 billion—as its debt had totaled when the decade began" (Schneider 1996: 164). Decades of industrialization also did nothing to reduce poverty for millions of Brazilians. Urbanization increased access to health care and education, but it also intensified social problems like violence and drugs.

BENEDITA DA SILVA

Throughout this book, I have introduced a variety of Brazilians—Chico Mendes, Lula, my neighbor Maria José—as a way of trying to get a handle on Brazil's complexity through the real-life experiences of individuals. Probably no single Brazilian so symbolizes the contradictions of contemporary Brazilian society as Benedita da Silva, who seems as full of paradoxes as Brazil itself (Silva 1997a).

In 1994, Benedita was elected to the Senate from the state of Rio de Janeiro, the first black woman senator in Brazilian history. Born in a *favela*, she was working on Rio's streets by the time she was 10 and was the only member of her family to learn to read and write, yet she occupies the second-highest elected office in Brazil. She grew up taking part in *Umbanda* rituals led by her mother; later she was active in the progressive Catholic Church's CEBs and was strongly influenced by liberation theology, but at 26 she joined the Pentecostal Assembly of God. Although Pentecostals have a reputation for social and political conservatism, Benedita is a member of the Workers' Party (PT), led by Lula. Criticized by both church and party members, Benedita proudly claims to be a "PTcostal" (Silva 1997a: 93).

Depending on how one looks at Benedita's life, one is filled with either hope or despair for Brazil's future. As a child, Benedita delivered clothes that her mother washed by hand to the home of Juscelino Kubitchek, who became the president responsible for building Brasília. Out of pity, his wife gave Benedita their daughter's hand-me-down clothes and even Benedita's first doll. Four decades later, Benedita served in Congress with the former president's daughter. A poor woman who has lived her whole life in Rio's *favelas*, she traveled to China in 1995, representing Brazil as a member of the largest delegation in attendance at the Fourth International Women's Conference. Benedita, who had 5 of her 12 bothers and sisters die as well as one of her own children, now uses her political position to push congressional investigation into the status of all Brazil's children.

Is Benedita's success a sign of how much has changed, that Brazil is overcoming race, gender, and class discrimination? Is Brazil modernizing? Thirty years ago, before the eruption of social movements demanding equality for women and blacks, it was hard to imagine the election of a poor black woman to the Brazilian Senate. Yet, the very fact that Benedita is such a *symbol* of the hopes and aspirations of poor, dark-skinned Brazilian men and women suggests how unusual her life has been; if her life were normal, no one would notice her. But she is unusual. Of the 559 congressional representatives, only 7 (1.3 percent) consider themselves black, although a majority of the population has some African ancestry (Silva 1997a: 128). When first elected to Congress, Benedita was part of a small minority of women (5.3 percent) even though there are more women than men in Brazil (UN 1991). How much has really changed?

THE FUTURE

> We have spent a long time being the country of the future. The future has arrived, the future is today, the future is now.
>
> *President Fernando Henrique Cardoso, August 13, 1997*

Brazilians have great faith in the future of their country. They believe that Brazil is destined to become one of the world's superpowers, playing the prominent international role befitting the world's fifth largest country. Brazilians feel that given the nation's enormous resources, both natural and human, it is only a matter of time until the nation realizes its boundless potential. More than three centuries of colonial domination, however, imposed handicaps, forcing Brazil to struggle far behind the world's more prosperous and powerful nations. In fact, if Brazil could somehow sustain the high economic growth rate of 1960–75 (4.2 percent), it would still take over 350 years to catch up to the leaders (Schaeffer 1997: 26).

GLOBALIZATION

President Cardoso believes that Brazil is ready to become the "country of the future," but what does that mean? What is this future world that Brazil expects to enter as a major actor? When sociologists look at world trends, they focus their attention on **globalization**, the increasingly tight economic, communication, and cultural linkages that are binding all nations into a single **world system** (Cockerham 1995: 32). Computers and satellites provide instantaneous worldwide communication. Factories are linked in a global production network. Without passports or visas, the art, literature, music, and food of the world's cultures flow across international borders. In this world system, no nation is independent; all are interdependent.

This global interconnectedness hit home to me in Brazil during September 1997 as I watched satellite images of the deaths and funerals of Princess Diana and Mother Teresa. All of Brazil was instantly aware of these sad events, and even though they took place on distant continents (Europe and Asia), we felt a part of them, mourning along with the people on the TV screen in London and Calcutta.

Technological advances seem inevitably to shrink our world, making communication, trade, and travel quicker, cheaper, and easier than at any other time in human history. Globalization appears unavoidable because the economic costs of not participating, of falling behind, are so high. But is increasing interdependence beneficial or harmful to a country like Brazil?

COSTS AND BENEFITS OF GLOBALIZATION

Many Brazilians are ambivalent about globalization. Throughout their country's history, tight linkages—from colonialism to the current foreign debt—have drained vital resources from Brazil. Brazil initiated industrialization only when international ties were weakened by the world depression following the stock market crash of 1929. Thus, Brazilians have reasons to be concerned that interdependence will not benefit everyone equally, that it will turn out to be just another word for dependence.

Openness to the world economy entails both risks and opportunities. For example, from 1985 to 1994, the value of U.S. manufacturing investments in Brazil doubled from $6.9 billion to $13.7 billion (SALA 1996). This investment helped sustain the Brazilian economy, but it also meant that profits generated in Brazil were more likely to be exported. The increasing role of transnational corporations also means that decision making is transferred to corporate headquarters in Tokyo, New York, and Bonn. In a globalized economy there is no guarantee that decisions will be made in Brazil's best interests.

Economic globalization also implies a globalization of culture. Every product is an expression of the culture where it was conceived. The marketing of transnational products, then, requires marketing the culture that makes the product desirable. Brazil's large population— 150 million—represents a huge potential market, and TNCs increasingly are globalizing Brazilian culture in a determined effort to sell their products. The increasing uniformity of products and culture across national boundaries has been referred to as the "McDonaldization" of societies (Cockerham 1995: 172).

To illustrate some of the complexities of globalization, three case studies are presented. The first looks at Brazil's attempt to improve its economic position in the world system by joining Mercosul, a regional trade bloc with Argentina, Paraguay, and Uruguay. The second examines the implications of the surprising success of Avon (the cosmetics and beauty-aid retailer) in the Brazilian Amazon. The third analyzes the apparently contradictory effects of television in Brazilian society.

Case Study 1: Mercosul

On March 26, 1991, representatives from Brazil, Argentina, Paraguay, and Uruguay signed the Treaty of Asunción, which established a "common market with free circulation of goods, services and productive means among its members" (quoted in Schvarzer 1998: 25). Brazilian leaders believed that Mercosul would promote further industrialization. By creating a larger consumer market (200 million in the four signing countries), industry could develop on a larger, more efficient scale.

To facilitate intraregional trade, 90 percent of the tariff and nontariff barriers to trade were eliminated between 1991 and 1994. Already in 1993, trade within Mercosul had quadrupled to $8 billion (Montenegro 1995: 32).

As a result, all members of Mercosul had doubled their total exports by 1996 (Schvarzer 1998: 26). The lower costs of trade have encouraged national industries to specialize production, creating economies of scale. For example, assembly plants have been located along the Argentina–Brazil border that produce cars with components manufactured in all four countries (Schvarzer 1998: 26).

Initially, Brazilian labor unions were suspicious of Mercosul. The one factor in production that was not allowed free movement across borders was labor. Union leaders feared that Mercosul would facilitate the movement of factories across borders in search of the cheapest, least organized workers. Therefore, unions demanded and received (in 1994) consultative representation to the Common Market Group (Montenegro 1995: 33). They also have pushed for the inclusion of a "social clause" in the Mercosul agreement that would guarantee equal labor rights (e.g., to organize and go on strike) and benefits (e.g., health and safety) across all four countries (Silva 1997b: 16). Workers for the first time created regional labor organizations (Schvarzer 1998: 27). As labor has learned how to work through and take advantage of Mercosul, workers have shifted from general opposition to cautious support with criticism of specific features of the agreement that harm their interests.

Mercosul is still too new to know what its long-term impact on Brazil will be. If it works as its creators hoped, Brazil will achieve a stronger position in the global economy through its regional ties. On the other hand, Brazil's economic competitors also are joining trade blocs (e.g., NAFTA with Canada, Mexico, and the United States), so Brazil may have to work harder just to stay in place. If Mercosul doesn't produce immediate benefits for all members, dissatisfaction could intensify to the point of sabotaging cooperation among the trading partners. If Mercosul appears to contribute to falling wages, it could provoke another round of nationalism, also undermining the trade agreement. For the moment, though, Brazil and the other three countries seem pleased with the increased trade and have even entered into additional trade agreements with Bolivia and Chile (Schuarzer 1998: 25).

Case Study 2: Avon in the Amazon

One of Avon's most successful sales representatives works in the Amazon. Eliana Maria Machado da Silva oversees approximately 1,000 Avon sales ladies in the northcentral Amazon. Eliana has done her job so well that she won an all-expenses-paid trip to Europe and the Middle East. The Amazon is a poor region, so to make sales, Avon representatives have to be creative, bartering Avon products for chickens or manioc flour to make sales; in mining camps, three grams of gold will get you a jar of Renew antiwrinkle cream.

With aggressive and creative salespeople like Eliana, Brazil has become Avon's largest non-U.S. market, with annual sales over $1 billion.

To make these sales, Avon has 478,000 representatives knocking on doors in Brazil. In comparison, there are only 200,000 soldiers in the Brazilian army. Avon's success has not gone unnoticed. Amway, which entered the Brazilian market in 1991, had 200,000 sales representatives four years later (Brooke 1995).

Avon products embody a particular cultural conception of beauty and hygiene. Thus, buying Avon implies acceptance of these cultural standards. The foreignness of these standards is evident when you consider that one of Avon's best-selling products in the Amazon is its deodorant Cool Confidence. The average midday temperature in Manaus (in the heart of the Amazon) is 85–90° with humidity over 60 percent (Draffen, McAsey, Pinheiro, and Jones 1996); in these conditions, even the world's most powerful deodorant offers little protection.

Imported conceptions of beauty are gaining ground in Brazil. In the past, to be *forte* (strong) was a compliment for women; to be *magro* (skinny) was cause for concern. These body perceptions were grounded in a context in which many people (women and men) have diets with insufficient calories. Thus, to be *forte* indicates prosperity and health, whereas to be *magro* suggests poverty and illness. These perceptions are changing rapidly, however. Soft drinks have long been popular in Brazil; but only recently have diet versions become fashionable, an ironic development in a country where many are thin, but not by choice.

If there are costs to Avon's activities in Brazil, there are benefits as well. Economically, Avon generates a significant number of employment opportunities for women. The flexible hours that are possible for sales reps make Avon an attractive way for women, who are also responsible for child and house care, to earn income. Avon representatives also are given more autonomy than comes with most jobs, which helps these women learn important business skills.

Brazilians have adopted many values and practices from other cultures, but in the process they are transformed into uniquely Brazilian forms. Thus, just because Avon products are adopted does not mean that they are used in the same way or for the same reason as they were intended. For example, an Avon skin cream is popular in the Amazon not for its moisturizing effects but because it acts as a mosquito repellent, a more critical product feature in the hot and humid climate.

Case Study 3: Television

When I first went to Brazil in 1974, I often watched television as a way to learn Portuguese. One of the most popular programs was reruns of the old *I Love Lucy* show; it was hilarious listening to Lucy speak fluent Portuguese with her Cuban husband Desi. *I Love Lucy* wasn't the only American show on Brazilian television. Another popular program was *Charlie's Angels*; the title in Portuguese was *As Panteiras* (The Panthers), apparently in deference to local religious sensibilities.

At the time, many Brazilians were quite concerned about the cultural imperialism of American television programming. In retrospect, the concern may have been exaggerated. Today an occasional U.S. program or movie is shown on Brazilian television, but the vast majority of programming is Brazilian. The most popular shows are *novelas*, serialized stories that run nightly (except Sunday) for several months. *Novelas* are so popular that they have been exported throughout Latin America, as well as to Europe, Africa, and even the People's Republic of China (Page 1995).

TV's pervasiveness in Brazilian culture has been severely criticized. In the movie *Bye-Bye Brazil*, a traveling troupe of circus performers realize that they are losing their audiences to television. Even in small rural communities, people preferred TV to live feats of dexterity and magic. In desperation, they head for the Amazon in search of a pre-TV Brazil. After traveling through the jungle, the circus performers come over the top of a hill and look down on the town that is their destination only to see with horror that the houses are topped by satellite dishes picking up programs beamed from São Paulo and Rio de Janeiro thousands of miles away. The implication is that the real, "live" Brazil has disappeared, replaced by a pseudo-Brazil that is watched rather than lived.

Others argue, however, that television has many positive effects in Brazil. Brazilian *novelas*, criticized for focusing on the lives and lifestyles of upper-class Brazilians, also have sparked public debate about some of the most serious issues facing Brazilian society—racism, political corruption, landlessness. TV may be socially isolating in the American context in which every family member has his or her own TV to watch his or her own shows, but in Brazil watching television is a social event that draws people together. During the 1982 World Cup, I didn't have a TV, so when I wanted to watch a game I walked down the street, stopping at the first house where I heard the game turned on. Always invited in, I not only was able to watch the games, but I also got to know my neighbors better.

Television is also criticized for discouraging reading. When TV arrived in Brazil, however, Brazilian culture was still largely preliterate. Printing presses had been outlawed into the 19th century by the Portuguese, and many Brazilians had insufficient literacy skills to make reading a frequent or desirable activity. In this context, TV did not discourage reading although it became the primary source of information. In fact, research indicates that Brazilians who watch TV are better informed about political and social issues and actually read more than those who don't watch television because TV has sparked their curiosity about the world (Kottak 1992).

CONCLUSION

At the end of the 20th century, Brazil is asserting itself economically and culturally in a world that is increasingly interconnected. Brazil's struggles with inequality and poverty make this transition a risky one.

If Brazil is drawn into international relations from a position of economic weakness, it may be taken advantage of as it has been in the past. Increased engagement in the world system, however, also holds out the possibility that Brazil will gain the technology and markets needed to fulfill its tremendous economic and cultural potential.

If sociologists are right about globalization, change is inevitable, but the impact of that change has yet to be determined. Will new opportunities be used to enhance the life chances of all Brazilians or will they be monopolized by a few? Only time will tell, but if the preceding case studies are indicative, the results may be ambiguous. Social reality is complex, and how we view the changes that Brazil is experiencing will depend on what is important to us.

BIBLIOGRAPHY

Alvarez, Sonia. *Engendering Democracy in Brazil: Women's Movements in Transition Politics.* Princeton: Princeton University Press, 1990.

Alves, Maria Helena Moreira. *State and Opposition in Military Brazil.* Austin: University of Texas Press, 1985.

Amado, Jorge. *Shepherds of the Night.* New York: Avon Books, 1966.

Americas Watch. "Urban Police Violence in Brazil." *Americas Watch* 5, no. 5 (1993), pp. 1–25.

Anuário–IBGE 1995.

Applebaum, Richard P.; and William J. Chambliss. *Sociology.* New York: Harper-Collins, 1995.

Astor, Michael. "Brazil Quiet as Evidence of Amazon's Demise Mounts." *Detroit News,* December 15, 1997. From website http://detnews.com/1997/9712/15/12150024.htm.

Baer, Werner. *The Brazilian Economy: Growth and Development.* 2nd ed. New York: Praeger, 1983.

Barbosa, Luiz C. "The 'Greening' of the Ecopolitics of the World- System: Amazonia and Changes in the Ecopolitics of Brazil." *Journal of Political and Military Sociology* 21 (1993a), pp. 107–34.

———. "The World-System and the Destruction of the Brazilian Rain Forest." *Review* 16, no. 2 (1993b), pp. 215–40.

Barros, Andréa; and Laura Capriglione. "*Soldados da Fé e Prosperidade.*" *Veja,* July 2, 1997, pp. 86–93.

Berryman, Phillip. *Liberation Theology.* New York: Pantheon Books, 1997.

Besse, Susan K. *Restructuring Patriarchy: The Modernization of Gender Inequality in Brazil, 1914–1940.* Chapel Hill: University of North Carolina Press, 1996.

Bodley, John H. *Victims of Progress.* Mountain View, CA: Mayfield, 1990.

Boff, Leonardo. *Church: Charism and Power.* New York: Crossroad, 1985.

Brooke, James. "In the Amazon, Guess Who's Calling?" *New York Times,* July 7, 1995, p. A4.

Brown, Diana De G. Umbanda: *Religion and Politics in Urban Brazil.* New York: Columbia University Press, 1994.

Bruschini, Cristina. "*O Trabalho da Mulher no Brasil: Tendências Recentes.*" Pp. 63–94 in *Mulher Brasileira É Assim,* ed. H. I. B. Saffioti and M. Muñoz-Vargas. Rio de Janeiro: Editora Rosa dos Tempos, 1994.

Brusco, Elizabeth E. *The Reformation of Machismo.* Austin: University of Texas Press, 1995.

Burdick, John. "The Lost Constituency of Brazil's Black Movements." *Latin American Perspectives* 25, no. 1 (1998), pp. 136–55.

Burns, E. Bradford. *A History of Modern Brazil.* 3rd ed. New York: Columbia University Press, 1993.

Cardoso, Fernando Henrique; and Enzo Faletto. *Dependency and Development in Latin America.* Berkeley: University of California Press, 1979.

Carranza, Maria. "*Saúde Reprodutiva da Mulher Brasileira.*" Pp. 95–150 in *Mulher Brasileira É Assim,* ed. H. I. B. Saffioti and M. Muñoz–Vargas. Rio de Janeiro: Editora Rosa dos Tempos, 1994.

Castro, Josué de. *Geografia da Fome.* 11th ed. Rio de Janeiro: Gryphus, 1992, p. 10+.

Cleary, David. *Anatomy of the Amazon Gold Rush.* Iowa City: University of Iowa Press, 1990.

Cockerham, William C. *The Global Society.* New York: McGraw-Hill, 1995.

Coelho, Marcos de Amorim. *Geografia do Brasil.* São Paulo: Editora Moderna, 1996.

Corral, Thais. "Brazil's Women-Run Police Stations Fight the Odds." *Ms,* November–December 1993, p. 18.

Corrêa, Marcos Sá. *"Ser Carioca Não É Crime."* *Veja,* September 8, 1993, p. 33.

Cunha, Euclides da. *Rebellion in the Backlands.* Chicago: University of Chicago Press, 1957.

Dantas, José. 1991. *História do Brasil.* São Paulo: Editora Moderna, 1991.

Davis, Shelton. *Victims of the Miracle: Development and the Indians of Brazil.* Cambridge: Cambridge University Press, 1977.

Degler, Carl. *Neither Black nor White: Slavery and Race Relations in Brazil and the United States.* New York: Macmillan, 1971.

Dimenstein, Gilberto. *Brazil: War on Children.* London: Latin American Bureau, 1991.

Dixon, William J.; and Terry Boswell. "Dependency, Disarticulation, and Denominator Effects: Another Look at Foreign Capital Penetration." *American Journal of Sociology* 102 (1996), pp. 543–62.

Draffen, Andrew; Chris McAsey; Leonardo Pinheiro; and Robyn Jones. *Brazil: Travel Survival Kit.* Oakland: Lonely Planet Publications, 1996.

Encyclopaedia Britannica Book of the Year. Chicago: Encyclopaedia Britannica, Inc., 1986.

ETAPAS. *Miséria Urbana: Uma Radiografia da Regiao Metropolitana do Recife.* Recife: ETAPAS, 1991.

Evans, Peter. *Dependent Development: The Alliance of Multinational, State, and Local Capital in Brazil.* Princeton: Princeton University Press, 1979.

———. *Embedded Autonomy: States and Industrial Transformation.* Princeton: Princeton University Press, 1995.

Firebaugh, Glenn; and Frank D. Beck. "Does Economic Growth Benefit the Masses? Growth, Dependence, and Welfare in the Third World." *American Sociological Review* 59 (1994), pp. 631–53.

Flynn, Peter. *Brazil: A Political Analysis.* Boulder: Westview Press, 1978.

Freyre, Gilberto. *The Masters and the Slaves.* New York: Alfred A Knopf, 1946.

———. *New World in the Tropics.* New York: Vintage, 1963.

Furtado, Celso. *The Economic Growth of Brazil.* Berkeley: University of California Press, 1963.

Gay, Robert. *Popular Organization and Democracy in Rio de Janeiro: A Tale of Two Favelas.* Philadelphia: Temple University Press, 1994.

Giles, Thomas S. "Forty Million and Counting." *Christianity Today,* April 6, 1992, p. 32.

Hanchard, Michael. *Orpheus and Power: The Movimento Negro of Rio de Janeiro and São Paulo, 1945–1988.* Princeton: Princeton University Press, 1994.

Harrison, Lawrence. *Development Is a State of Mind: The Latin American Case.* Lanham, MD: Madison Books, 1985.

Hess, David J. *Samba in the Night: Spiritism in Brazil.* New York: Columbia University Press, 1994.

Hewlett, Sylvia. *The Cruel Dilemmas of Development: Twentieth Century Brazil.* New York: Basic Books, 1980.

Higley, John; and Michael G. Burton. "The Elite Variable in Democratic Transitions and Breakdowns." *American Sociological Review* 54 (1989), pp. 17–32.

Hoffman, Helga. "Poverty and Prosperity: What Is Changing?" Pp. 197–232 in *Social Change in Brazil, 1945–1985: The Incomplete Transition*, ed. E. L. Bacha and H. S. Klein. Albuquerque: University of New Mexico Press, 1989.

Horowitz, Irving Louis. *C. Wright Mills: An American Utopian*. New York: Free Press, 1983.

IBGE (see Instituto Brasileiro de Geografia e Estatístico).

Instituto Brasileiro de Geografia e Estatístico (IBGE). *Anuário Estatístico do Brasil*. Rio de Janeiro: IBGE, 1995.

Jeffrey, Paul. "Targeted for Death." Pp. 154–62 in *Fighting for the Soul of Brazil*, ed. K. Danaher and M. Shellenberger. New York: Monthly Review Press, 1995.

Jesus, Carolina Maria de. *Child of the Dark: The Diary of Carolina Maria de Jesus*. New York: Mentor Books, 1962.

Jornal do Comércio. "*Povo Lincha Três Assassinos no Bairro.*" September 5, 1993.

Kahil, Raouf. *Inflation and Economic Development in Brazil 1946–1963*. Oxford: Clarendon Press, 1973.

Kay, Cristóbal. *Latin American Theories of Development amd Underdevelopment*. London: Routeledge, 1989.

Kemper, Vicki; and Larry Engel. "A Prophet's Vision: The Life of Dom Helder Cámara." *Sojourners* 16, no. 11 (1987), pp. 12–15.

Kottak, Conrad. *Assault on Paradise: Social Change in a Brazilian Village*. 2nd ed. New York: McGraw-Hill, 1992.

Kuczynski, Pedro-Pablo. *Latin American Debt*. Baltimore: Johns Hopkins University Press, 1988.

La Tour, Marcus. "Extractive Reserves: Economic and Social Alternatives for the Tropical Rainforest." Pp. 123–29 in *Fighting for the Soul of Brazil*, ed. K. Danaher and M. Shellenberger. New York: Monthly Review Press, 1995.

Lernoux, Penny. *The Cry of the People*. New York: Penguin, 1980.

———. "In Common Suffering and Hope: The Base Community Movement in Brazil." *Sojourners* 16, no. 11 (1987), pp. 22–28.

Lipset, Seymour Martin. *American Exceptionalism: A Double-Edged Sword*. New York: W. W. Norton, 1996.

Lombardi, Cathryn L.; John V. Lombardi; and K. Lynn Stoner. *Latin American History: A Teaching Atlas*. Madison, WI: University of Wisconsin Press, 1983.

Lovell, Peggy A.; and Charles H. Wood. "Skin Color, Racial Identity, and Life Chances in Brazil." *Latin American Perspectives* 25, no. 3 (1998), pp. 90–109.

Marger, Martin N. *Race and Ethnic Relations: American and Global Perspectives*. 4th ed. Belmont, CA: Wadsworth, 1997.

Margolis, Mac. "The Invisible Issue: Race in Brazil." *Ford Foundation Report*, summer 1992, pp. 3–7.

Martin, David. *Tongues of Fire: The Explosion of Protestantism in Latin America*. Cambridge: Basil Blackwell, 1989.

Matta, Roberto da. *Conta de Mentiroso: Sete Ensaios de Antropologia Brasileira*. Rio de Janeiro: Editora Rocco Ltda., 1993.

Maybury-Lewis, David. *Indigenous Peoples, Ethnic Groups, and the State*. Boston: Allyn and Bacon, 1997.

McDonald, Ronald H. and J. Mark Ruhl. *Party Politics and Elections in Latin America*. Boulder: Westview, 1989.

Mintz, Sidney. *Sweetness and Power: The Place of Sugar in Modern History*. New York: Penguin, 1985.

Montenegro, Marcelo. "Labor and Mercosur." *NACLA Report on the Americas* 28, no. 6 (1995), pp. 32–33.

Morel, Mário. *Lula, o Metalúrgico: Anatomia de uma Liderança.* Rio de Janeiro: Editora Nova Fronteira, 1989.

Nelson, Sara. "Constructing and Negotiating Gender in Women's Police Stations in Brazil." *Latin American Perspectives* 23, no. 1 (1996), pp. 131–48.

Neuhouser, Kevin. "The Radicalization of the Brazilian Catholic Church in Comparative Perspective." *American Sociological Review* 54 (1989), pp. 233–44.

———. "Stable Dependency and Unstable Regimes: A Comparative Historical Analysis of Transitions Between Democratic and Authoritarian Regimes in South America, 1945 to 1985." Ph.D. dissertation, Department of Sociology, Indiana University, 1990.

———. " 'Worse than Men': Gendered Mobilization in an Urban Brazilian Squatter Settlement, 1971–1991." *Gender and Society* 9, no. 1 (1995), pp. 38–59.

———. "Transitions to Democracy: Unpredictable Elite Negotiation or Predictable Failure to Achieve Class Compromise?" *Sociological Perspectives* 41 (1998), pp. 67–93.

———. " 'If I had Abandoned My Children': Mobilization and Commitment to the Identity of Motherhood." *Social Forces* 77, no. 1 (1998), in press.

New Internationalist. "Jungle of Myths." Pp. 101–2 in *Fighting for the Soul of Brazil,* ed. K. Danaher and M. Shellenberger. New York: Monthly Review Press, 1995.

O'Donnell, Guillermo; and Phillipe C. Schmitter. *Transitions from Authoritarian Rule: Tentative Conclusions about Uncertain Democracies.* Baltimore: Johns Hopkins University Press, 1986.

Page, Joseph A. *The Brazilians.* Reading, MA: Addison-Wesley, 1995.

Pang, Eul-Soo. "Agrarian Change in the Northeast." Pp. 123–39 in *Modern Brazil: Elites and Masses in Historical Perspective,* ed. M. C. Conniff and F. D. McCann. Lincoln: University of Nebraska Press, 1989.

Perlman, Janice. *The Myth of Marginality.* Berkeley: University of California Press, 1976.

Perney, Linda. "The Rubber Tappers under Fire." Pp. 109–12 in *Fighting for the Soul of Brazil,* ed. K. Danaher and M. Shellenberger. New York: Monthly Review Press, 1995.

Pearce, David; and Norman Myers. "Economic Values and the Environment of Amazonia." pp. 383–404 in *The Future of Amazonia: Destruction or Sustainable Development,* eds. David Goodman and Anthony Hall. London: McMillan, 1990.

Pinheiro, Flávio. *"A Revolução das Mulhers." Veja,* August 13, 1997, p. 14.

Powers, John. "Fighting for the Soul of Brazil." *Los Angeles Times Magazine,* March 27, 1994, pp. 15–20, 46.

Ramos, Graciliano. *Barren Lives.* Austin: University of Texas Press, 1969.

Revkin, Andrew. *The Burning Season.* Boston: Houghton Mifflin, 1990.

Ribeiro, Darcy. *O Povo Brasileiro: A Formação e o Sintido do Brasil.* São Paulo: Companhia das Letras, 1995.

Roberts, Bryan. *Cities of Peasants: The Political Economy of Urbanization in the Third World.* Beverly Hills: Sage, 1978.

Roddick, Jackie. *The Dance of the Millions: Latin America and the Debt Crisis.* London: Latin American Bureau, 1988.

Rostow, W. W. *The Stages of Economic Growth.* 3rd ed. Cambridge: Cambridge University Press, 1990.

Saffioti, Heleieth. *"Violência de Gênero no Brasil Contemporâneo."* Pp. 151–86 in *Mulher Brasileira É Assim,* ed. H. I. B. Saffioti and M. Muñoz-Vargas. Rio de Janeiro: Editora Rosa dos Tempos, 1994.

SALA (see *Statistical Abstract of Latin America*).

Schaeffer, Robert K. *Understanding Globalization.* Lanham, MD: Rowman and Littlefield, 1997.

Schemo, Diana Jean. "Brazilians Chained to Job, and Desperate." *New York Times,* August 10, 1995, pp. A1, A6.

Scheper-Hughes, Nancy. *Death without Weeping: The Violence of Everyday Life in Brazil.* Berkeley: University of California Press, 1992.

Schneider, Ronald M. *Brazil: Culture and Politics in a New Industrial Power.* Boulder, CO: Westview, 1996.

Schvarzer, Jorge. "Mercosur: The Prospects for Regional Integration." *NACLA Report on the Americas* 31, no. 6 (1998), pp. 25–27.

Schwartz, Mary Ann; and BarBara Marliene Scott. *Marriages and Families: Diversity and Change.* Englewood Cliffs, NJ: Prentice Hall, 1994.

Schwerin, Karl H. "The Indian Populations of Latin America." Pp. 39–53 in *Latin America, Its Problems and Its Promise,* ed. J. K. Black. Boulder: Westview, 1991.

Scott, James C. *Weapons of the Weak.* New Haven, CT: Yale University Press, 1985.

Shapiro, Helen. "The Mechanics of Brazil's Auto Industry." *NACLA Report on the Americas* 29, no. 4 (1996), pp. 28–33.

Silva, Benedita da. *Benedita da Silva: An Afro-Brazilian Woman's Story of Politics and Love.* Oakland: Food First, 1997a.

———. "Benedita da Silva: Community Activist and Senator, Brazil." *NACLA Report on the Americas* 31, no. 1 (1997b), pp. 13–16.

Silva, Nelson do Valle. *"Distância Social e Casamento Inter-racial no Brasil."* Estudos *Afro-Asiáticos* 14 (1987), pp. 54–84.

Silva, Nelson do Valle; and Carlos Hasenbalz. *Relogões Raciais no Brasil Contemporâneo.* Rio de Janeiro: Instituto Universitário de Pesquisas do Rio de Janeiro: Rio Fund Editora, CEAA, 1992.

Silveiro Bueno, Francisco da. *Minidicionário da Língua Portuguesa.* São Paulo: Editora Lisa, 1992.

Sindicato dos Trabalhadores Domésticos na Área Metropolitina da Cidade do Recife. O Valor Social do Trabalho Doméstico. Recife: Sindicato dos Trabalhadores Domésticos na Área Metroplotina da Cidade do Recife and SOS Corpo, 1996.

Skidmore, Thomas. *Politics in Brazil, 1930–1964.* New York: Oxford University Press, 1967.

———. *Black into White: Race and Nationality in Brazilian Thought.* New York: Oxford University Press, 1993.

Skole, David; and Compton Tucker. "Tropical Deforestation and Habitat Fragmentation in the Amazon: Satellite Data from 1978 to 1988." *Science* 260 (1993), pp. 1905–910.

Smelser, Neil J. *Comparative Methods in the Social Sciences.* Englewood Cliffs, NJ: Prentice-Hall, 1976.

Smith, Brian H.; and Frederick C. Turner. "Survey Research in Authoritarian Regimes." Pp. 795–814 in *Statistical Abstract of Latin America,* ed. J. W. Wilkie and A. Perkal. Los Angeles: UCLA Latin American Center Publications, 1984.

Smith, Christian. *The Emergence of Liberation Theology.* Chicago: University of Chicago Press, 1991.

———. "The Spirit and Democracy: Base Communities, Protestantism, and Democratization in Latin America." Pp. 245–63 in *Crossing Currents: Continuity and Change in Latin America,* ed. M. B. Whiteford and S. Whitehead. Upper Saddle River, NJ: Prentice Hall, 1998.

Smith, Sheldon; and Philip D. Young. *Cultural Anthropology: Understanding a World in Transition*. Boston: Allyn and Bacon, 1998.

Smith, T. Lynn. *Brazil: People and Institutions*. Baton Rouge: Louisiana State University Press, 1963.

Soares, Maria Clara Couto. "Who Benefits and Who Bears the Damage Under World Bank/IMF-Led Policies." Pp. 8–16 in *Fighting for the Soul of Brazil*, ed. K. Danaher and M. Shellenberger. New York: Monthly Review Press, 1995.

Souto Maior, Mário. *A Mulher e o Homen na Sabedoria Popular*. Recife: 20–20 Comunicação e Editora, 1994.

Stark, Rodney; and James C. McCann. "Market Forces and Catholic Commitment: Exploring the New Paradigm." *Journal for the Scientific Study of Religion* 32 (1993), pp. 111–24.

Statistical Abstract of Latin America. Los Angeles: UCLA Latin American Studies Center, various years.

Stepan, Alfred. *The Military in Politics*. Princeton: Princeton University Press, 1971.

Stevens, Evelyn. "*Machismo* and *Marianismo*." *Science* 10 (1973), pp. 57–63.

Tapia, Andrés. "Why Is Latin America Turning Protestant?" *Christianity Today*, April 6, 1992, pp. 28–29.

Telles, Edward E. "Racial Distance and Region in Brazil: Intermarriage in Brazilian Urban Areas." *Latin American Research Review* 28, no. 2 (1993), pp. 141–62.

Therborn, Goran. "The Travail of Latin American Democracy." *New Left Review* 113–14 (1979), pp. 71–109.

Tinoco, Pedro; and Virginie Leite. "*A Máscara da Lei*." *Veja*, September 8, 1993, pp. 22–25.

Torloni, Hilário. *Estudos de Problemas Brasileiros*. 10th ed. São Paulo: Livraria Pioneira Editora, 1977.

Torregrossa, Lusita Lopez. "*Escândolo* in Brazil." *Vanity Fair*, February 1993, pp. 132–38, 159–64.

Twine, France Winddance. *Racism in a Racial Democracy: The Maintenance of White Supremacy in Brazil*. New Brunswick, NJ: Rutgers University Press, 1998.

UN. *The World's Women 1970–1990: Trends and Statistics*. New York: United Nations, 1991.

———. *The World's Women: Trends and Statistics*. New York: United Nations, 1995.

UN-ECLA. *The Process of Industrialization in Latin America: Statistical Annex*. New York: UN-ECLA, 1966.

Veja, October 1, 1986.

Veja. "*Especial Mulher: A Grande Mudonga no Brasil*." August/September 1994.

Vita, Alvaro de. *Sociologia da Sociedade Brasileiro*. 2nd ed. São Paulo: Editora Ática, 1991.

Wearne, Phillip. *Return of the Indian: Conquest and Revival in the Americas*. Philadelphia: Temple University Press, 1996.

West, Robert C. "Aboriginal and Colonial Geography of Latin America." Pp. 34–80 in *Latin America and the Caribbean: A Systematic and Regional Survey*, ed. B. C. Blouet and O. M. Blouet. New York: John Wiley & Sons, 1993.

agregado   Someone who is aggregated or added in. Individuals are incorporated into a household and treated like kin. Historically, large landowners attracted many *agregados* under their protection. An informal way to adopt children.

aldeias   Communities established by the Jesuits to evangelize and protect Indians from enslavement.

aperreado   Intense state of nervousness and anxiety. Victims may tremble or become unable to make decisions. It is caused by a combination of the emotional stresses of poverty and the nerve damage caused by chronic malnutrition.

caatinga   Indigenous name for the thorny scrub forest of the dry *sertão* meaning "white forest." In the intense tropical sunlight, the leafless landscape appears white.

caboclos   A person of mixed Indian and European ancestry. Within *Umbanda*, *caboclos* are Indian spirit guides.

Candomblé   Name given the African spiritism practiced around Salvador, Bahia.

Caranguejo   Recife *favela* where the author lived and worked (1980–83) and has continued to conduct research. The name for this community of approximately 4,000 residents comes from the little crabs—*caranguejos*—that live in the marshy area.

casa   House or home. The domestic sphere (world of family, friends) viewed as women's proper place.

CEBs   Portuguese acronym for "ecclesiastical base communities." At the movement's peak, there were an estimated 80,000 CEBs in Brazil. Each CEB is a small group of lay Catholics who study the Bible together and apply it to the political and economic problems of their community and Brazilian society.

compadre/comadre   Godparents; individuals chosen to sponsor an infant's baptism. It is an important way to extend networks by establishing fictive kin relations with nonfamily members.

conhecer   Portuguese verb for "to know"; applied to subjective knowledge or knowledge gained through experience.

dar um jeito   To "find a way." This phrase indicates that everything is possible, regardless of rules. There is always a way around the obstacle to one's goal. The person with *jeito* is admired for creatively finding solutions to impossible situations.

delegacias da mulher   A police station entirely staffed by women and dedicated to investigating crimes against women. In 1985, Brazil became the first country to establish such a station.

dona de casa   Title for married women (*dona* for short); the "owner of the house," indicating that the house is a female domain. Poor urban women use this cultural status to claim possession of the house in *favelas* where no one has legal title.

embranquicimento   Light skin is more socially desirable in Brazil than dark, so Brazilians pursue "whitening" by marrying a lighter-skinned spouse and claiming the whitest color category possible.

empates   Literally, a "tie," as in a scoreless soccer match. In the Amazon, it refers to a standoff between rubber tappers and landowners attempting to cut down the rain forest. The rubber tappers surround the workers who have been hired to cut down trees and disarm them by taking their chain saws.

favelas   Urban communities created by the invasion of unused land, often in marginal areas such as hillsides or swamps. Residents resist police attempts to remove them and must struggle to access public services like water, electricity, and health care.

fazendeiros   Large plantation owners who have economic, political, and social power over workers and their families.

forte   "Strong"; an indication of health and prosperity; a desirable trait in the context of poverty and malnutrition.

guarana   Soft drink made from a red Amazonian berry.

industria da seca   The "drought industry." Millions of dollars flow though government drought programs, becoming a major source of jobs and income. The money for drought prevention and support of drought victims has been captured mostly by the *fazendeiros*.

irmão/irmã   "Brother" and "sister." Terms used by Protestants to indicate that they are now part of a new church family.

Kardecismo   Spiritism based on teachings received from the druid spirit Alan Kardec, combining elements of European positivism with Christian ethics and eastern reincarnation. Especially popular among educated middle-class groups in southern Brazil.

litoral   The coastal region of Brazil.

machismo   Traditional Brazilian gender ideology defining ideal male behavior as aggressive, sexual, and dominant. Men are to be active in the public world of politics and work; their family role is to earn income to sustain the household.

mãeinha   "Little mother," or mommy. Mothers and daughters use this term of endearment with each other, socializing daughters to see themselves as becoming mothers.

magro   "Skinny"; a negative body image because it indicates sickness or poverty.

marginais   "Marginals"; the poor, usually dark-skinned *favela* residents, assumed to be uncivilized. They are ignored, feared, and devalued by wealthy Brazilians.

marianismo   Traditional Brazilian gender ideology that models ideal female behavior on Mary, the mother of Jesus. Women are to be passive, spiritual, and submissive. Women's spirituality, wisdom, however, gives them considerable power within the home.

movimento   "Action"; Brazilians prefer crowds and noise to quiet and solitude. Thus, urban centers are viewed as more desirable than outlying suburbs. As a result, the U.S. urban pattern of poor inner cities and wealthy suburbs is reversed in Brazil.

mulato   Person of mixed African and European ancestry.

mulher brava   Woman considered to be brave or wild because she acts in aggressive male ways. She deviates from gender norms, but she is admired because male behavior is more valued.

mulherinha   "Little woman"; derogative term for males, implying that they are acting like a woman and may be gay.

novelas   Serialized television dramas shown six evenings a week and continuing for several months. These are a very popular form of entertainment in Brazil and have been exported to countries in Europe, Africa, Latin America, and Asia.

obedecer mas não cumprir   "To obey but not fulfill." Rules can be technically obeyed even as their spirit or intent is broken. Given the overbureaucratization of the Brazilian state, almost everything violates some rule, so ways are found to avoid the law's intent, yet stay (barely) within the letter of the law.

orixás   African deities. The *orixás* were given names of Catholic saints to conceal the continued practice of African religion. The *orixás* possess their devotees, temporarily taking control of their bodies, opening communication between the supernatural and natural worlds.

pardo   General racial category, commonly translated as "brown." Applies to the numerous Brazilians of mixed ancestry.

preto velho   Literally, "old black." In *Umbanda*, the *preto velho* is a wise, old spirit of a former slave.

quilombos   Communities of escaped slaves that survived the determined efforts of the Portuguese to destroy them. The most famous was Palmares, which survived for nearly a century with a population of 20,000.

rua   "Street"; the public world of interaction with strangers, making it a risky but interesting place. A male sphere.

saber   "To know"; applies to the objective knowledge of facts.

saudade   Combines two emotions that seem contradictory in English: the "sad joy" of remembering something good; something distant or gone "that is at the same time both sad and soft" (Silveira Bueno 1992).

se Deus quiser   "If God wills." Traditional expression of fatalism, the belief that whatever happens is what God wants and nothing humans do can change it.

sem terras   Landless rural residents. They have organized a national movement to claim land that is not being used.

seringueiros   Rubber tappers who have harvested the Amazon rain forest for generations, using sustainable methods that allow the jungle to renew itself.

sertanejos   The inhabitants of the dry *sertão*.

sertão   Semi-arid region in the interior of northeast Brazil that is subject to periodic devastating droughts.

Umbanda   Uniquely Brazilian spiritism; combines belief in *orixás* with the spirits of Brazilians and foreigners. In style, it is more similar to African spiritism than to *Kardecismo*.

Xangô   Name given to the African spiritism practiced around Recife, Pernambuco.

SOCIOLOGY GLOSSARY

applied sociology   Application of sociological knowledge in real world settings.

assimilation   Process by which an ethnic group loses its distinctiveness, adopting the dominant culture of the society.

boom and bust   Alternating economic cycles in which rapid growth is followed by stagnation, often caused by the lack of diversified production and dependence on external markets.

bureaucracy   Hierarchical organization in which behavior and decisions are determined by a formally articulated set of rules.

capital goods industrialization   Industrialization strategy that focuses on the production of the machinery and industrial products used in the manufacture of consumer goods.

charismatic authority   Authority based on the personal qualities of a leader, which are perceived by followers to be so exceptional that the leader must be obeyed.

class   Ranking in a stratification system based on access to economic resources or a particular position in the system of production (e.g., workers versus capitalists).

client   Person who seeks economic resources by offering labor and loyalty.

coerced labor   Workers who are legally or physically forced to work, as in slavery or debt peonage.

colonialism   Political and economic domination of one society by another.

conversion   Adoption of a new meaning system (beliefs, values, norms), creating a new sense of self and often restructuring social relations (who one relates to and how one relates).

culture   Learned behavior, beliefs, knowledge, and values shared by members of a society.

deepening   Attempt to move beyond import substitution industrialization to the manufacture of capital goods (goods that are inputs to industry rather than consumer goods).

dependence   Economic relationship between nations in which the economic growth of a country is controlled by other countries.

dependency theory   Latin American economic theory that argues that the region's development has been inhibited and distorted by its economic relations with Europe and North America.

development   Economic progress measured either by economic statistics like gross domestic product or in social terms of the overall well-being of the population.

deviance   Behavior or beliefs that violate social norms.

discrimination   Unequal treatment, whether intentional or not.

division of labor   Assignment of different work to specific groups, most commonly by gender, race/ethnicity, and age.

doing gender   Idea that gender is not determined by biology but is the performance of a cultural script. Not all situations are covered by the script, so improvisation is sometimes allowed. Not everyone is equally capable or willing to follow the script, however, so not everyone "does" their gender equally well.

domestic sphere   World of home and family.

double day   Working women face two workdays, one of paid work outside the home and one of unpaid work inside the home.

elite   Small group occupying the most powerful economic and political positions in society.

ethnic group   A subpopulation within a society that shares a particular cultural legacy (language, religion, history).

extended family   Parents, children, and multigenerational kin.

family of orientation   Family into which one is born.

family of procreation   Family formed by marriage.

female-headed household   Household in which a woman has primary responsibility for decision making. It's generally assumed that when an adult male is present, the woman is *not* the head, though she may be a more central and permanent member of the household.

feminine movements   Social movements seeking resources women need to perform traditional gender roles. In Brazil, they demanded day care, running water, and medicine that women need to be mothers.

feminist movements   Social movements seeking to transform gender roles. In Brazil, they sought improvement in women's treatment by addressing issues like wage discrimination and domestic abuse.

fertility rate   Average number of children that a woman gives birth to during her lifetime.

festival of reversal   A ritual that reverses or inverts the normal social order by making the powerless powerful, the dirty clean, the private public.

fictive kinship   Establishment of relationships in which people treat one another as if they were kin. In Brazil, the most common forms are *compadres/comadres* and *agregados*.

foraging societies   Societies that produce food by hunting and gathering.

gender   The cultural expectations about how women and men should be.

gender ideologies   Cultural norms defining proper female and male behavior. Deviance from these norms is often punished.

gender role   Set of behaviors linked to being male or female.

gender-role identity   Sense of self based on the performance of gendered behaviors.

genocide   Acts resulting in the destruction of a people.

globalization   Process binding nations into a single world system by expanding ties of communication, markets, and culture.

gross domestic product (GDP)   Measure of the total value of goods and services produced within a country.

horticultural societies   Societies that produce food on small garden plots with simple hand tools.

hypodescent   Racial classification system in which children are assigned the race of the parent with the lowest racial status. This classification system is used in the United States but not in Brazil.

ideal culture   Beliefs about what values and behavior should be in a culture.

import substitution industrialization (ISI)   Industrialization process that replaces imported manufactured goods (mainly mass consumer goods) with locally produced manufactured goods.

indigenous populations   Populations predating the arrival of Europeans.

infant mortality   The number of deaths of babies during the first year of life per 1,000 live births.

informal economy   Economic activity outside government control; includes prohibited activities (stealing, prostitution, drugs) and activities failing to conform to government regulations (unlicensed business, undocumented workers, child labor).

institutional discrimination   Denial of equal access to resources, rights, or opportunities based on the impersonal practices and policies of organizations and social groups.

land reform   Significant change in the pattern of land ownership to achieve more efficient production or equitable distribution.

life chances   Differential probability of experiencing particular states (marriage, employment, illness) or gain certain resources (income, power, education) during one's life.

life expectancy   The average number of years that a group of infants is expected to live.

matrilineal   Family that is traced through the mother's line.

mechanization   Process of replacing human labor with machinery.

messianic movements   Religious movements in which people seek a supernaturally powerful person to destroy evil and establish a just society.

modernization theory   Theory that predicts that Third World countries like Brazil are following in the path of industrialized countries like the United States and Japan.

mortality rate   Average annual number of deaths per 1,000 people in the population.

myth of marginality   The belief that poor urban Brazilians are culturally and economically marginal. Rejected by sociologist Janice Perlman in her book of the same title (1976).

natural increase   Population growth caused by a higher birth than mortality rate. Excludes growth due to migration.

nongovernmental organization (NGO)   A private organization active in development, human rights, and environmental issues.

norms   Expectations of behavior that are shared within a group.

patron   Wealthy individual who provides economic resources to clients in exchange for labor and loyalty.

patron–client relations/system   Exchange of the client's loyalty and labor for the resources of the patron. The exchange is unequal, as the patron wields considerable power over the client.

popular Catholicism   Everyday folk beliefs and practices in Brazil, contradicting or modifying the official orthodox religion.

prejudice   Negative belief or attitude toward a group.

primary products   Goods that are largely unprocessed (i.e., raw) like mineral and agricultural goods.

private sphere   See *domestic sphere.*

public sphere   Economic and political world where interaction with nonfamily members or friends is the norm.

race   Socially constructed category grouping people based on the perceived similarity of some physical traits.

race mixing   Process in which racial intermarriage produces intermediary racial groups.

racial democracy   Racial interaction on the basis of equality.

racism   Prejudice or discrimination against people based on their membership in a particular racial category.

real culture   The actual values, beliefs, and behaviors in a culture; may be very different from the ideal culture.

reproductive labor   Work that ensures the survival of humanity day to day and generationally; includes bearing children, nurturing children and adults, cooking, and cleaning.

social movement   Group-based attempt to change some social, economic, or political feature of society.

socialization   Process by which individuals are taught the appropriate behaviors, values, and knowledge of a group.

stereotype   Assumption that all members of a particular group share some characteristics.

stratification   Hierarchical divisions within society.

structures   Patterned social, economic, and political relations that persist over time and constrain behavior.

sustainable development   Use of natural resources that doesn't diminish resource availability for future generations.

syncretism   The blending of two different belief systems.

transnational corporation (TNC)   Firm whose research, production management, and marketing span the globe.

underemployed   People, like most poor Brazilians, who work but receive inadequate hours or pay.

urbanization   Geographic movement from countryside to city; involves movement to a radically different social environment.

weapons of the weak   The poor and powerless cannot directly confront those who take advantage of them, so they engage in indirect and covert resistance that will not provoke retaliation.

women's movements   Social movements whose primary participants are women.

world system   An integrated economic system that increasingly incorporates the entire world.

NAME INDEX

SUBJECT INDEX